Waterway Walks around Birmingham

David Perrott

Published by Sigma Leisure – an imprint of
Sigma Press, 1 South Oak Lane, Wilmslow, Cheshire SK9 6AR, England.

British Library Cataloguing in Publication Data
A CIP record for this book is available from the British Library.

ISBN: 1-85058-406-0

Typesetting and Design by: Sigma Press, Wilmslow, Cheshire.

Cover: all photographs by Chris Rushton. Top left: Wolverhampton; top and bottom right: Stratford; bottom left: Amblecote.

Printed by: Interprint Ltd., Malta.

Preface

It is no secret that the greatest concentration of canals in the country is in and around Birmingham. This city really took water transport to its heart, and is still a splendid area for canal exploration. You will find that many of the original features still remain, and you won't need a boat to be able to appreciate them. Stout shoes and a raincoat will do.

Virtually every canal has a tow-path (more correctly 'towing path') alongside, making for easy, level walking. Even flights of locks have only gradual ascents and descents. I am always fascinated by the generally unobtrusive routes chosen by the early canal engineers, passing through open country well hidden in river valleys, and more often than not sneaking through, or just beside, quiet villages. Entries into towns are usually inauspicious, with lots of back yards and allotments to admire. Locks, bridges, aqueducts, docks, tunnels, disused arms, pumping stations, toll booths and reservoirs are passed with great regularity, creating a great deal of interest. Sturdy cast iron and cosy red brick assembled with small scale utilitarian charm are constant reminders of a world constructed on a human scale, where a couple of men and a horse would transport a load at walking pace, with no noise and minimal pollution.

They would stop for rest and refreshment at canal-side pubs, with an adjacent stable for their horses. Many of these traditional Black Country hostelries are still there for us to enjoy - indeed the pubs in this area are particularly good. Beer is not over-prices and there is plenty of good real ale from local breweries. Food is served up in decently sized helpings and is always good value. Canal pubs especially often retain many original features, and have a good warming coal fire. The barmaids are usually friendly and welcoming and call you 'luv'. As a visitor, you soon begin to feel at home. If you are a resident, count your blessings.

Of course a thriving city such as Birmingham can't afford too much time wallowing in nostalgia. There has been some very thorough re-development in the centre, and it won't be to everyone's taste. I try to keep it all in perspective by imagining, when I am walking, what an intrusion the building of canals must have been upon a largely rural population who would never have experienced such monumental works. Remember, prior to the canal age, no roads, no railways, and no proper river navigations. Then it all changed.

The Black Country Museum in Dudley celebrates all of this, and should not be missed. Surrounded by busy roads, a charming collection of 18th and 19th century buildings and relics has been assembled, with mine visits, tram rides, a fairground and boat trips into the Dudley Tunnel to keep you and your family amused.

I hope you enjoy these walks. Take your time, explore, visit the pubs (assuming you are not driving home) and leave the present day to look after itself, while you think of times past.

David Perrott

Contents

Introduction

The Walks

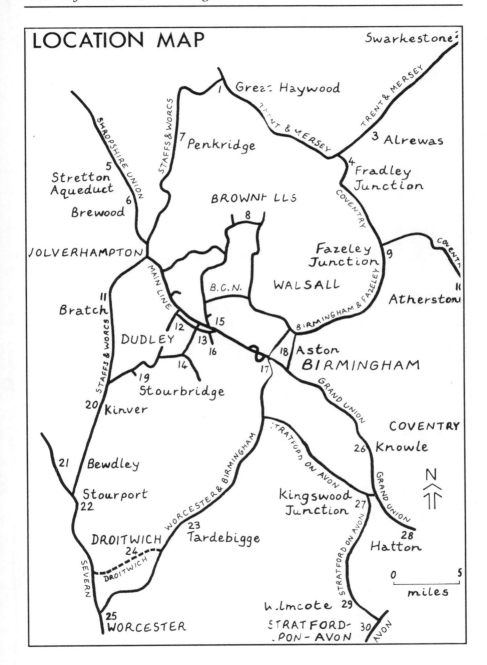

INTRODUCTION

When the Duke of Bridgewater opened the canal linking his coal mines at Worsley with the expanding population of Manchester in 1765, it heralded the start of 'the canal age'. This means of transporting goods along artificial waterways was to dominate inland transport for almost 200 years, until the coming of the railways. Built at a time when roads were non-existent, and the only means of transporting goods was either by pack horse, or by boat along rivers (subject to drought, flood and blockages caused by mill-owners), the capacity and reliability of the canal boat was a revolution. Large tonnages of coal could now be moved with relative ease to wherever they were needed, fuelling the furnaces and machinery of the Industrial Revolution.

Others quickly grasped the potential for economic benefit which this new mode of transport could bring. Among them was Josiah Wedgwood (1730-95), the famous potter, who, with his friends Thomas Bentley and Erasmus Darwin, promoted the building of a canal to link the rivers Trent and Mersey. Construction began in 1766 and the project was completed in 1777. It was an immediate success, with vast tonnages of raw materials and finished goods being moved along it. The Trent & Mersey Canal is visited on Walks 1, 2, 3 & 4. The Staffordshire & Worcestershire Canal was built at the same time, to provide a link from the Trent & Mersey to the River Severn, and onwards to the great port of Bristol. Unlike the Bridgewater Canal, which was built to a wide gauge, able to take craft up to 70ft by 14ft, these later canals, built to a narrower gauge due to the need for economy and the vagaries of water supply, were unable to compete when the railways came on the scene a century later. The narrowboat, which could carry a 30 ton load pulled by one horse and was remarkable in its time, became hopelessly inadequate in later years.

The Staffordshire & Worcestershire Canal is visited on Walk 1, where it joins the Trent & Mersey at Great Haywood Junction; on Walk 7; Walk 11, where it negotiates the unusual Bratch Locks; Walk 20, where it passes the famous beauty spot of Kinver; and Walk 22. Here it joins the River Severn at Stourport, the only town in the country built as the direct result of the construction of a canal.

Whereas Manchester can justly claim to be the birthplace of British canals, it is equally true that it was the industrial City of Birmingham which really took canal transport to heart. In 1768 the Birmingham Canal Company decided to build a route from Aldersley, on the Staffordshire & Worcestershire Canal, to Birmingham. Completed in 1772, this canal, which passed through an area of great mineral wealth and developing industry, was assured of success. The Birmingham Canal is visited on Walk 12, where it passes close to the wonderful Black Country Museum. The original Birmingham Main Line, and the New Main Line, which was built by Thomas Telford between 1825 and 1838, pass side by side through the Galton Valley. Pressure of traffic and congestion on the old route made it necessary to build a parallel route, and you can visit them both on Walk 15. Walk 17 starts at Gas Street Basin. Also known as the Worcester Bar, this was where the Birmingham Canal met the Worcester & Birmingham Canal. So jealous were the companies of maintaining their water supplies, these two canals were physically separated by a bar, across which goods had to be transhipped.

Gangs of itinerant workers, known as navigators (from which we get the term 'navvy', as applied to road builders) dug the canals by hand, using the most rudimentary tools. As they travelled, they sought relaxation in the local inns and taverns, and were well known for their rowdy behaviour, which often shocked the rural communities they passed through. Early canals were often built to follow the lines of contours, thus keeping the need for locks, tunnels and embankments to a minimum. The Birmingham Old Main Line is an excellent example of this technique. Thomas Telford, who came onto the scene when the canal age was well advanced, favoured the taking of more direct routes, with vast cuttings and massive embankments, a method known as 'cut and fill'. His New Birmingham Main Line shortened the original route by 7 miles (11.3km). The Shropshire Union Canal was also built by Telford, and is explored on Walks 5 and 6. You will notice immediately how straight the line of the canal is, and the mighty scale of the earthworks. As if to compensate for his massive intrusions into the land, Telford adorned his canals with fine architectural features.

By 1790 canal mania gripped the country – many schemes which received the Royal Assent were never built, others which were built were poorly planned and badly engineered. Shortage of water was a constant problem, and supplies were protected by 'stop locks', such as that on Walk 18. Cut-throat competition resulted in toll-cutting battles. Many canals never made a penny profit, and were soon abandoned. The Droitwich Canals, on Walk 27, are just such an example. They are currently being restored.

The Birmingham Canal Company eventually became the Birmingham Canal Navigations, a network measuring almost 160 miles (257km) in length, and fed by hundreds of short arms, basins and wharves. Rival canals were amalgamated into this network: the Dudley Company in the south, and the Wyrley & Essington in the north. Closures have reduced the BCN to about 100 miles (160km), but any further contractions are unlikely. The Dudley Canals connected the Staffordshire & Worcestershire Canal to the Worcester & Birmingham Canal by means of the now-closed Lapal Tunnel (3795 yards [3470 m]), with a branch to the Main Line through Dudley Tunnel. These routes are visited on Walks 8 and 14. Netherton Tunnel was built parallel to the Dudley Tunnel to relieve congestion. You can enjoy an exciting walk through all 3027 yards (2768m) of this on Walk 13.

The Wyrley & Essington Canal was the subject of an unfortunate closure in 1954 when the section to the east of Ogley Junction, which linked with the Coventry Canal at Huddlesford Junction 7 miles (11.3km) away, was abandoned. Part of the Wyrley & Essington is followed on Walk 8. It soon becomes apparent that this is an early contour canal, contrasting with the straight-as-a-die Cannock Extension Canal, completed in 1863, which is followed at the start of the walk. You will also see Chasewater, a vast canal feeder reservoir, and one of the most successful.

Another such reservoir is passed on Walk 23, beside the daunting flight of 30 Tardebigge Locks. Situated just below the summit, water was pumped up from this reservoir to maintain the level at the top. The old pump house still stands by the canal. Pumping stations are also passed at Smethwick, on Walk 15, and at Titford, on Walk 16, where water is fed to the highest navigable pound (length of canal) in Birmingham.

One of the most consistently profitable canals in Britain was the Coventry, visited on Walks 9 and 10. Construction began in 1768, and soon the coalfield at Bedworth was linked with Coventry. The whole route was not completed until 1790, in a joint scheme with the Birmingham & Fazeley Company. Meeting with the Oxford Canal at Hawkesbury, the link was now made with Britain's other great river, the Thames, and thus on to London.

The capital's new trade route to Birmingham was not entirely satisfactory, however, as it involved a journey up the River Thames and along the Oxford Canal, a tortuous contour route. This prompted the building of the Grand Junction Canal, now the Grand Union. Originally built to the narrow gauge, it was widened in the 1930s in an attempt to revive canal carrying. Two of the impressive new flights of locks built during modernisation are visited on Walks 26 and 28.

The Grand Union joins the Stratford-on-Avon Canal at Kingswood Junction. On Walk 27 you will notice a clear difference in scale between these two waterways, the Stratford Canal having a quaintness that disappeared from the Grand Union with modernisation. One of the prettiest waterways, the Stratford Canal's proximity to the sights associated with William Shakespeare makes Walks 29 and 30 particularly interesting.

Walk 30 includes a stretch of the River Avon, recently restored to navigation after many years of neglect. This river empties into the River Severn, which is visited on Walk 21, at the handsome old river port of Bewdley, and on Walk 25, where Worcester Cathedral is dominant.

During the 19th century the railway age began. Carrying heavier loads at greater speeds, the canals were hard pressed to compete. Engineering improvements and toll cutting could not halt the inevitable decline, and soon closures became commonplace. In some instances the canals were bought by the railway companies, drained and used as track-beds for the more modern form of transportation, but more often than not they were left to fall into decay. Commercial carrying over the whole canal network ended in the early 1960s, and although there have been laudable attempts to revive it on the larger, industrial waterways, it has never made a significant impression. History now seems to be repeating itself with the lack of support for railways and the emphasis on road transport, whatever the environmental cost. But if you are lucky, you may still see the odd working boat, perhaps at Atherstone (Walk 10), operated by enthusiastic supporters of water transport.

It is, of course, holiday craft that now predominate, and this explosion of leisure interest has brought about the preservation of the canal system, and the restoration of many long-disused canals. British Waterways, local councils, The Inland Waterways Association and local societies all work to improve and enlarge upon the available navigable miles. What was once seen as an eyesore, a muddy ditch or a danger, can now be transformed into an amenity for boaters, walkers, joggers, fishermen, bird-watchers and naturalists to enjoy.

At canal junctions, boatyards and canal-side pubs you will usually find many moored boats. Look out for those traditional craft maintained by enthusiasts. Often painted with roses and castles, and embellished with bold lettering, they are a reminder of the times when whole families lived on board, crammed into their cosy boatman's cabin, furnished with lace and brass. Perhaps you will see one underway and towing a butty (an un-powered narrowboat), the distinctive sound of its single cylinder Bolinder diesel, a slow *thunk-thunk-thunk*, announcing its imminent arrival and giving you plenty of time to get the camera ready.

PLANTS AND WILDLIFE

There is something very special about walking beside water. The sparkle of waves caught by the sun, the reflection of trees and sky and the ripples caused by fish on a summer's evening have a special magic which can add a new dimension to your walking. These features remain whether you are in the heart of the countryside or the heart of a city, such as Birmingham. Water also has another attraction – it acts as a natural magnet for wildlife, and supports a wide variety of very special plants which enjoy the wet conditions.

Amongst the first to appear in the spring are clumps of pond sedge, four feet tall and covered with dark brown flower spikes. Later, in May, the showy yellow flag iris appears, colonising wet and marshy places and filling them with colour. A similar plant, but with much less conspicuous flowers, is the sweet flag, so named because its leaves have a sweet smell when crushed. It was used to cover floors in medieval times, the scent providing relief from other, less desirable, smells.

Hiding in the shade you will find marsh marigolds and the shiny yellow lesser celandine. Often you will walk right past them, unnoticed under the canal or river bank, by the water's edge. Later in the year shaggy purple loosestrife, the bell-shaped flowers of comfrey in white, purple and pink, the massive marsh woundwort, the blue greater skullcap, the white gypsywort, the yellow bur marigold, mauve water mint and greenish-white angelica all add to the variety of colours. Please remember, none of these wild flowers should be picked – leave them where they are to grow and propagate.

Out of the main channel used by boats you will often see water lilies. These are rooted in the canal or river-bed and produce fine yellow or white flowers. The circular floating leaves and tangled underwater stems provide the perfect hiding place for fish, and these in turn attract many anglers each weekend who love to sit by the water's edge in the hope of catching a fine specimen.

The canal water in the Birmingham area is generally pretty clean, and all the common species of coarse fish – roach, dace, bream, perch, tench, pike – are to be found. Stand quietly by the waterside on a summer evening and you may see the ripples as the smaller fish rise to take insects and flies which have landed on the surface.

You will have to get closer to the water, in a quiet spot, to see water skaters gliding over the surface, and water boatmen, swimming upside-down just below the surface. Dragonflies dart from bank to bank, dipping to the surface of the water and then settling on a waterside plant. They begin life in the water, the larvae being noted for their voracious feeding habits. Also starting its life in the water is the caddis fly. The larvae of this interesting creature live in little tubes of grit and leaves which they cement together. Water spiders spend their whole life in the water, but they breathe air trapped as a bubble in a tiny web between their legs and abdomen.

With such a profusion of plants, trees and insects, it is not surprising that many birds live by, or visit, the water. The most common ducks are mallards and Aylesburys. They happily interbreed and will expect to share your sandwiches. The male mallard is a very handsome bird with a bottle-green head, white collar and grey body. Their mates are a dull, mottled brown.

If you disturb a heron it will often fly a hundred yards or so along the water and land, so that you can again come close and cause it to repeat the whole procedure. This can happen three or four times until this large grey bird loses patience and flies off over the trees with its characteristic slow noisy flaps of the wings.

A streak of sapphire in the corner of your eye is usually the first sighting of a kingfisher, perhaps the most exotic of British birds. They fly too quickly to see their red underside and feet, and flash of white behind the eye. Having caught a fish in a shallow dive, the kingfisher will beat it to death on a branch and swallow it head first, so that the fins and scales don't get caught in its gullet. These fine birds have often been seen on the Stratford-on-Avon canal, so look out for them on Walk 27.

USEFUL ADDRESSES

The relevant **Weathercall** telephone forecast can be obtained on 0891 500411 (charge).

Tourist information is available from the following addresses. They all provide information on accommodation, events, attractions and entertainments.

Bewdley	St George's Hall, Load Street Car Park, Bewdley, Worcestershire DY12 2EQ. Tel: 0299 404740.
Birmingham	2 City Arcade, Birmingham, West Midlands B2 4TX. Tel: 021-643 2514.
Birmingham Airport	West Midlands B26 3QJ. Tel: 021-767 7145.
Burton upon Trent	Town Hall, Burton upon Trent, Staffordshire DE14 2EB. Tel: 0283 508000.

Droitwich	St Richard's House, Victoria Square, Droitwich, Worcestershire WR9 8DS. Tel: 0905 774312.
Dudley	39 Churchill Precinct, Dudley, West Midlands DY2 7BL. Tel: 0384 250333.
Kidderminster	Severn Valley Railway Station, Comberton Hill, Kidderminster, Worcestershire DY10 1QX. Tel: 0562 829400.
Kinver	Traveller's Joy, 47 High Street, Kinver, West Midlands DY7 6HE. Tel: 0384 872940.
Lichfield	Donegal House, Bore Street, Lichfield, Staffordshire WS13 6NE. Tel: 0543 252109.
National Exhibition Centre	West Midlands B40 1NT. Tel: 021-780 4321.
Redditch	Civic Square, Alcester Street, Redditch, Worcestershire B98 8AH. Tel 0527 60806.
Stafford	The Ancient High House, Greengate Street, Stafford ST16 2JA. Tel: 0785 40204.
Stratford-upon-Avon	Bridgefoot, Stratford-upon-Avon, Warwickshire CV37 6GW. Tel: 0789 293127.
Tamworth	Marmion House, Lichfield Street, Tamworth, Staffordshire B79 7BZ. Tel: 0827 311222.
Warwick	The Court House, Jury Street, Warwick CV34 4EW. Tel: 0926 492212.
Wolverhampton	18 Queen Square, Wolverhampton, West Midlands WV1 1TQ. Tel: 0902 312051.
Worcester	The Guildhall, High Street, Worcester WR1 2EY. Tel: 0905 726311.

The navigation authority for the majority of waterways visited on these walks is:

British Waterways   Peels Wharf,Lichfield Street, Fazeley, Staffordshire B78 3QZ. Tel: 0827 252000.

The Upper Avon is administered by:

The Upper Avon Navigation Trust   Avon House, Harvington, Evesham, Worcestershire.

The Droitwich Canals are administered by:

The Droitwich Canals Trust   1 Hampton Road, Droitwich, Worcestershire WR9 9PA.

The Inland Waterways Association (IWA) campaigns for the restoration, retention and development of inland waterways in the British Isles, and their fullest commercial and recreational use.

IWA   114 Regent's Park Road, London NW1 8UG. Tel: 071-586 2510/2556.

ABOUT THE WALKS

There is a short introduction to each walk, together with the length and a grading so that you can choose walks to suit your interests and abilities. The numbers (1, 2, etc) refer to numbered points on the sketch maps. The letters (A, B, etc) identify points of interest which are described separately from the walk directions; these places are also on the sketch maps.

SAFETY

Walking beside water is relaxing and always interesting, but young children must be closely supervised at all times, especially near locks, where the water is deep, the stonework slippery when wet, and there is sometimes exposed machinery.

Dog owners are also reminded that if they allow their animal to bound around unsupervised, it can cause accidents. Please keep your dog on a lead at all times near the water.

RIGHTS OF WAY

All the routes in this book follow rights of way, well-established concessionary paths or tow-paths. Some tow-paths are not dedicated rights of way, but it is British Waterways' policy to continue to allow their use on a permissive basis for public recreation.

The Walks

Walk 1:
Tixall and
Great Haywood

4 miles (6.4km). Moderate

A woodland walk with fine views over the valley of the River Sow is followed by a splendid section of towpath and a unique canal feature. After crossing an ancient bridge you can, if you wish, visit one of the most architecturally pleasing of stately homes. The return to the start is through Shugborough Park, where follies, built in classical Greek and Roman style, enliven the landscape.

The Route

1. Start from Cold Man's Glade car park, which is about half way between Stafford and Rugeley on the A513, not far from the entrance to Shugborough Working Farm Museum. Bus numbers 823 & 825 between Stafford and Lichfield (for information phone 0785 223344) stop here.

   Turn left from the car park, then left again to pass a wooden barrier. Continue up the track. Walk to the left around a raised reservoir enclosed by railings and take a wide path off to the left. You soon reach a clearing. Take the right-hand path on the far side to walk downhill. When you join the road at Milford, turn right.

2. Pass the main entrance to Shugborough Hall and turn right along the road beside it. Join the canal down steps to the left of the bridge. Walk with the water on your left.

3. At Great Haywood Junction, go under the bridge and turn right. Pass the first lock, go under the bridge then immediately turn right to join a drive through a gap in a stone wall. Turn left to walk away from the canal.

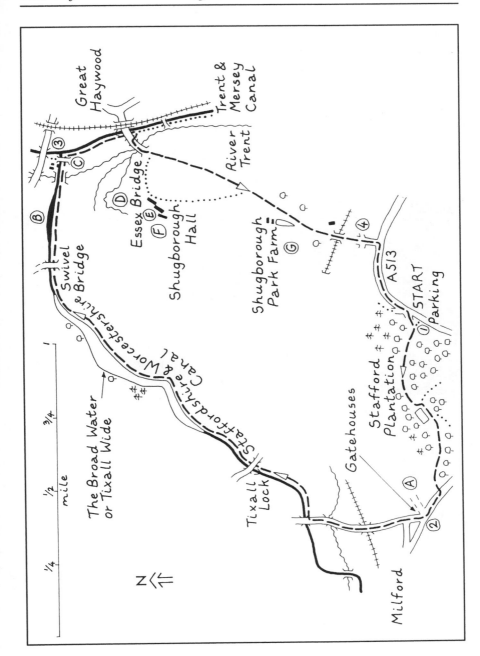

4. After crossing a railway, the drive bends to the right. Maintain your direction here, going through the gate ahead. Go through the next gate to emerge at the main road. Turn right to return to the start.

Tixall Lock and cottage, on the Staffordshire and Worcestershire Canal

Places of Interest

A. This is the main entrance to Shugborough Park and Hall, guarded by the handsome Milford Lodges, built around 1800. They were desig-ned by Samuel Wyatt, who was also responsible for many of the finer features of Shugborough Hall (see E, below).

B. Tixall Wide, on the Staffordshire & Worcestershire Canal, is over-looked by the massive Tixall Gatehouse, built *circa* 1575 for Sir Walter Aston. It is one of the largest gatehouses in the country, three stories high, richly decorated with Roman, Ionic and Corinthian columns, and topped with four tall turrets. Tixall Hall no longer exists – but it must have been quite magnificent to merit a gatehouse as impressive as this. The canal was probably widened to resemble a lake, since it was in full view of the hall.

C. The Staffordshire & Worcestershire Canal crosses the River Trent on an aqueduct, before joining the Trent & Mersey Canal at Great Haywood Junction. The brick bridge here has a particularly elegant sweeping arch, and was the subject of a very popular and well-used photograph taken by the canal historian Eric de Maré.

D. Essex Bridge, which crosses the River Trent, is a packhorse bridge probably dating from the 16th century. It has 14 arches, is just 4 feet (1.2m) wide and not broad enough for a horse and carriage. The Anson family, then owners of Shugborough Hall (see E below), had a wider bridge built about 100 yards (90m) downstream, so that they did not have to walk 300 yards (275m) to church each Sunday.

E. Shugborough Hall was built in 1693, and subsequently enlarged by Thomas Anson (1695-1773). The wings, designed by Thomas Wright, were added around 1748. These were later extended by Athenian Stuart. In 1794, Samuel Wyatt added the eight columned portico, giving the façade a unity it would otherwise lack.

The original village of Shugborough once stood in the 900 acre park. It was demolished so that the grounds could be landscaped, and the inhabitants were rehoused in the handsome cottages in Trent Lane, Great Haywood. The site of the old village is now occupied by the Arch of Hadrian, which contains the busts of Admiral Lord Anson and his wife. It was built to celebrate Anson's circumnavigation of the world in 1740-4, and his distinguished naval career, which included the capture of a Spanish treasure galleon and culminated in his becoming First Lord of the Admiralty in 1751. The younger brother of Thomas Anson, Lord Anson died in 1762, having supplied most of the funds to enlarge the hall.

The interior of Shugborough Hall is richly decorated, with exquisite Rococo plasterwork by Vassalli, and splendid collections of 18th-century ceramics, silverware, paintings and French furniture.

With fluctuating fortunes and crippling death duties, the house was finally transferred to the National Trust during the 1960s. Managed by Staffordshire County Council, it is still the home of Patrick Lichfield, the photographer, who is 5th Earl and a member of the Anson family.

The parkland and gardens are well worth exploring at any time of year. They contain eight monuments built as landscape features, with such glorious names as the 'Lantern of Diogenes' and 'Tower of the Winds'. The Hall and Park are usually open daily 11am – 5pm (4pm from October – Easter). Telephone 0889 881388. Admission charge, café and shop.

F. Housed in what were the servant's quarters, the Staffordshire County Museum gives an intriguing view of the other side of life at Shugborough – that of the 'downstairs' staff and workers who were needed to make the estate function. You can see the scullery and kitchen, the laundry, the butler's pantry and the school-room, together with galleries containing formal displays. There is also a collection of horse-drawn vehicles. Opening times are the same as the hall.

G. The Park Farm, designed by Samuel Wyatt, contains an agricultural museum, a working mill and a rare breeds centre. Traditional country skills, such as bread making, butter churning and cheese making are demonstrated. Opening times are the same as the hall.

Walk 2:
Swarkestone

4 miles (6.4km). Easy

The bridge at Swarkestone, where this walk starts, is a well-known landmark. The Summer House passed on the walk reminds us of this area's past associations with the Harpur family, and an old canal junction provides another, more recent, focus of interest. The return is beside the River Trent.

The Route

1. Start from the Crew & Harpur pub, by the bridge in Swarkestone, near the junction of the A5132 and A514. You can park beside the Ingleby road, by the bridge. Bus numbers 68 & 69 from Derby stop by the bridge (for information phone 0332 292200).

   Walk across the road from the pub and follow the public footpath signposted away from the riverside path, towards the church. Cross a stile and continue with a fence on your right. Cross a stile by a metal gate to join the road at the church. Turn left to walk around the edge of the churchyard. Ignore a stile into the churchyard, but cross the stile to your left. Turn right and walk with a stone wall on your right. Maintain your direction to join a wooden fence on your right. Walk past The Summer House on your left.

2. Go through the metal gate closest to the stone wall around The Summer House and continue ahead to go through a gap in the hedge, to a metal gate. Go through it and over a bridge. Look for the prominent white railings of a canal bridge across the field to the right. Walk directly to the bridge. Join the canal and walk with the water on your right.

3. Leave the canal up steps at bridge 16 and turn left. Carefully cross the main road and continue along Brookfield into Barrow upon Trent. Go

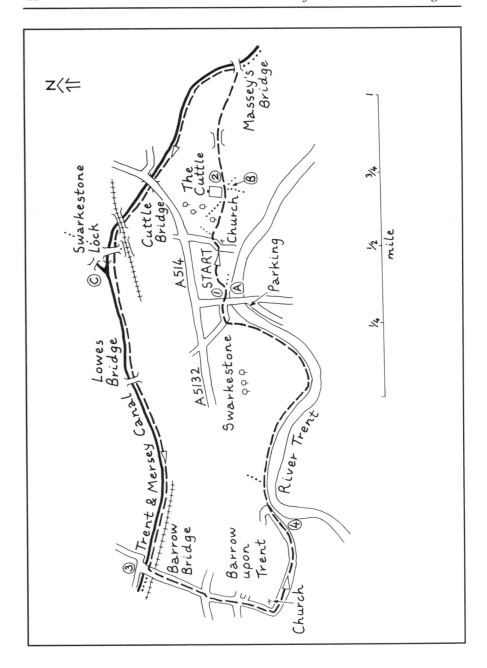

down Church Lane and follow the road as it curves left past the church, with the River Trent to the right..

4. When the road ends, follow the public footpath signposted ahead, going through a squeeze stile. Follow the path over a foot-bridge, and walk with the river on your right. Approaching Swarkestone Bridge, cross a stile, then look for a lane between Leylandii cypress trees. Go down this lane, cross a stile, turn right and emerge at a road. Turn right again to return to the start.

Places of Interest

A. The original bridge and causeway were about three quarters of a mile (1.2km) long, and were built during the 13th and 14th century. Seventeen of these original arches remain. The present bridge, with its five handsome arches, dates from 1801.

B. This peculiar building, known as The Summer House or Grandstand, overlooks a square enclosure called The Cuttle. Of Jacobean origin, it was part of the Harpur family estate. It is thought that bull-baiting and other performances were watched here, although alternative suggestions for its use have included some kind of bowling green. The Harpur family moved to Calke, a few miles to the south, following the demolition of their mansion after the Civil War. The pub, The Crew & Harpur, by the bridge, stands as another reminder of their past involvement in the village, as do many monuments in the church.

C. This old canal arm, now used for moorings, is all that remains of the Derby Canal. Built in 1796, it ran via Derby to join the Erewash Canal at Sandiacre. Long abandoned, the old toll house which remains at the junction serves as a clubhouse for the local boat club.

Walk 3:
Alrewas

3 miles (4.8km) Easy

An outward route past a narrow lock and a pretty weir, and then alongside the River Trent, provides an invigorating start to this splendid walk. The return, beside the Trent & Mersey Canal, is punctuated by visits to two churches: at Wychnor, and in the attractive village of Alrewas.

The Route

1. Alrewas is signposted off the A38 between Lichfield and Burton upon Trent. There is easy roadside parking by the Post Office and war memorial. Bus numbers 112 from Burton and 23 from Lichfield stop here (for information phone 0785 223344).

   Walk from the Post Office to pass the Crown Inn on your right. Turn right at Park Road. After about 100 yards (90m), turn left into a roughly-surfaced road, which becomes a track. Cross a fence stile beside a gate and walk over to Alrewas Lock. Cross another fence stile by a gate to the right of the lock, and continue, always keeping the water on your left. Go through a gate and cross numerous stiles to arrive at a main road.

2. Turn left and walk to where the turn off to Wychnor is signposted. Turn left to join the canal by Wychnor Lock, and continue with the water on your left. Visit Wychnor Church by crossing the stile which appears to your right just after the bridge below the church. Rejoin the canal and continue, crossing six towpath foot-bridges.

3. Do not cross the very long foot-bridge before the lock, but look for a fence stile down to the right. Cross it, turn left and walk to the bridge to the right of the large mill building. Cross the fence stile and then the bridge, and continue ahead. Pass a metal gate and cross another bridge to emerge at a road. Turn right.

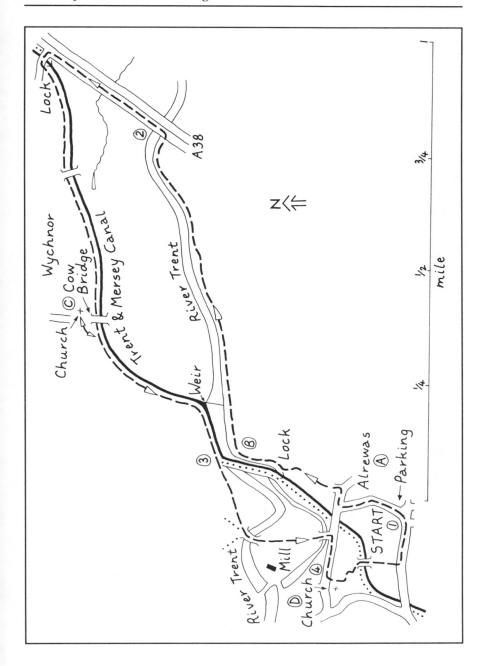

4. Go through the white wicket-gate to enter the churchyard, and visit the church. Walk past the little bowling green to your left to emerge at the canal towpath through a metal gate. Turn left and cross the foot-bridge. Continue ahead to the road. Turn left to return to the start.

Places of Interest

A. With many timber-framed cottages and quiet back lanes, Alrewas is a pretty village, well situated in the valley of the River Trent. The large buildings of Cotton Mill, to the north, indicate the river's proximity. The present mill dates from the mid 19th century, having been built on the site of an earlier mill. Alrewas is a corruption of 'Alder Wash', and is pronounced 'olrewus'. Alders once grew in profusion here, and gave rise to the basket weaving industry for which the village was famous. It is now a favourite venue for anglers and Sunday afternoon visitors.

B. The Trent & Mersey Canal and the river cross here, sharing a common course. Navigating a boat on this stretch can be tricky when the river is in spate.

C. The red brick tower of the pretty church of St Leonard's overlooks the canal and river. Built in Early English Decorated style, parts of it date from around 1200, although the tower was probably added in the 17th century. Wychnor is a tiny farming settlement, standing above ancient earthworks on the flood plain of the river.

D. All Saints Church stands in a peaceful churchyard beside the canal. Remodelled over the years, it has two Norman doorways, an Early English chancel and a 14th-century west tower. Look for the old leper window, now filled with modern stained glass. Victims of this unfortunate disease could watch the services through the window, without infecting the congregation.

All Saints Church, Alrewas: on St George's Day

Walk 4:
Fradley Junction

4.5 miles (7.2km). Easy

Easy level walking with plenty of canal interest make this a relaxing tour. The junction at Fradley, an imposing pub and the nearby locks provide one of those focal points peculiar to the inland waterways network. As a result there are always plenty of brightly coloured narrowboats to admire.

The Route

1. Fradley is signposted off the A38 between Lichfield and Burton upon Trent. Start from the Post Office in the village centre, where there is easy roadside parking.

   With your back to the Post Office, walk to the right. Fork left by the school and continue, to join the canal at Fradley Bridge. Walk with the water on your left.

2. Turn right at Fradley Junction. Pass Junction Lock, cross the bridge and walk with the canal now on your right. Continue through a gate at Keepers Lock.

3. Cross bridge 49 at Bagnall Lock and turn right to walk along the fenced track. Go under the road bridge and turn left through a wooden gate. Walk along the left-hand side of the field to emerge through a gateway at a road. Cross the fence stile opposite and walk diagonally right to cross another stile. Maintain this direction to leave the field through a gap in the hedge, crossing a little foot-bridge. Walk with the hedge on your left.

4. Join a road through a gap in the hedge, turn right and walk about 50 yards (45m). Cross the first stile on your left, just beyond a house. Walk with the hedge on your right. Cross a stile beside a gate, cross the foot-bridge opposite and walk straight across the field. Walk

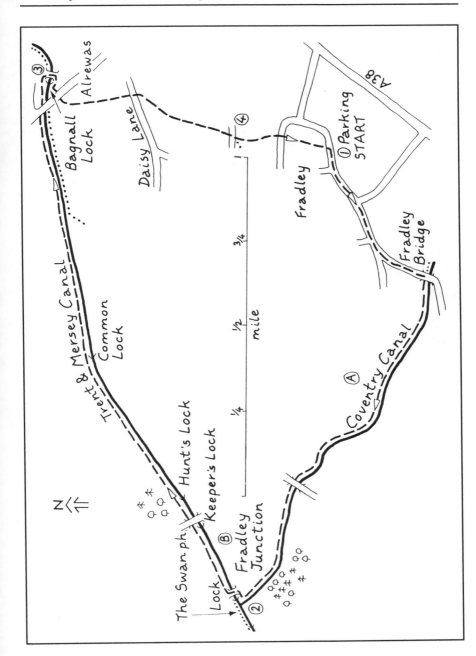

along a rough track between houses to join the road. Turn right to return to the start.

Places of Interest

A. The Coventry Canal was built to link the prosperous town of Coventry with the new Grand Trunk Canal, now known as the Trent & Mersey. Although one of the most consistently profitable canals in Britain, paying a dividend to its shareholders until 1947, the Coventry Canal got off to a difficult start following its enabling Act of 1768. Initial construction from Coventry to the coalfields at Bedworth was completed in 1769, but by the time it reached Atherstone (see Walk 10) in 1771, all the capital had been spent, and the engineer, James Brindley, sacked. It finally reached Fradley in 1790, sharing part of its route with the Birmingham & Fazeley Canal.

B. The Coventry Canal joins the Trent & Mersey at Fradley Junction. Many of the classic waterways ingredients can be seen here: a handsome pub with old stables, a flight of locks, various types of bridges, a British Waterways maintenance yard with a crane, and lots of brightly-coloured narrowboats.

Walk 5:
Stretton Aqueduct &
Belvide Reservoir

6 miles (9.7km). Moderate

*There are initially some fine views over rich farmland from Thomas Telford's
high canal embankments. Then, after enjoying a more intimate tree-lined
cutting, the return route passes Belvide Reservoir, much loved by bird-watchers,
before rejoining the canal at Brewood.*

The Route

1. Start from The Bridge Inn, Brewood. The village is on a minor road
   signposted off the A449 and the A5, west of Cannock. Centro buses
   numbers 3 & 12 from Wolverhampton stop here (021-200 2700 for
   details). Considerate roadside parking is available. This route can be
   linked with Walk 6, which also starts here.

   Go through the white wooden gate opposite The Bridge Inn to join
   the canal. Walk with the water on your left. After crossing Stretton
   Aqueduct, go under the next bridge and immediately leave the canal
   by walking up a path to the right. Turn right and cross the bridge.

2. Go through a wooden gate and turn left along a farm road. Follow
   the right-hand hedge to cross a stile in a corner, ignoring the gates.
   Walk with a hedge on your right, following the path through trees.

3. Emerge from the trees at a stile. Cross it. Veer left over the field to a
   stile to the right of a gate in the corner. Cross the stile and walk with
   the hedge on your left. Go through two gates at White Gate Farm.
   Fork left to climb another gate and emerge at the A5 road.

4. Turn left for 50 yards (45m), then carefully cross the road to take the
   track signposted 'Private Road, No Vehicles'. After crossing the

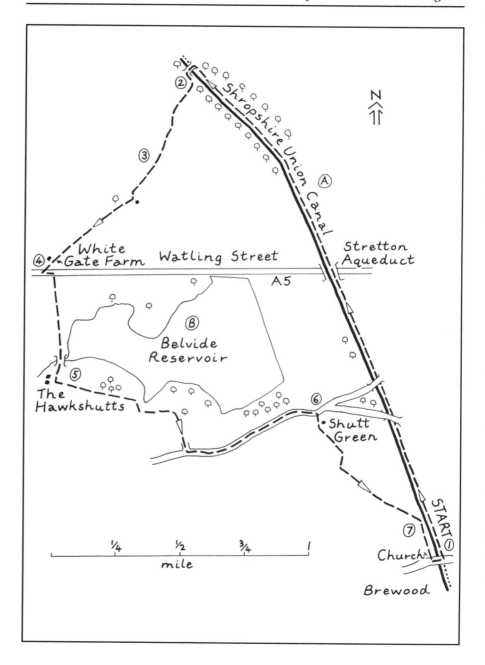

bridge over the tip of Belvide Reservoir, take the second stile on your left, just before Hawkshutts Farm. Walk with a fence on your left.

5. Cross a stile and walk with a wire fence on your left. Cross the next stile and walk diagonally right across a rough field, climbing a small embankment to a pond. Cross a stile and an overflow channel to the left. Walk down through bushes to cross a stile on your right. Walk ahead across a field to cross a stile opposite. Turn right along a track. Turn left at the road.

6. Turn right at Leafields Farm. Walk between the buildings to go through a metal gate, then cross the stile beyond it. Continue diagonally left over the field to a stile beside a post, just to the right of an obvious clump of trees. Cross it and turn right. When you are level with a line of four trees to your left, turn left to follow the line of the trees, to eventually join a track which comes in from your right.

7. Walk alongside a hedge on the left. Go through a wooden gate and turn right, to walk to the road. Turn left to return to the start.

Places of Interest

A. Telford's canals are characterised by their direct routes, deep cuttings, high embankments, and a contemptuous disregard of contours – so the quaintness of canals built earlier is missing. As if to compensate, Telford added fine architectural features for us all to enjoy.

B. Belvide Reservoir was built as a feeder for the canal. It is now a nature reserve.

Walk 6: Brewood

3.5 miles (5.6km) Easy

This walk starts in a deep, tree-lined cutting, where, on a sunny day, dappled light falling onto the water is delightful. After crossing the distinctive Avenue Bridge, there is a fine view of Brewood from one of the surrounding hills.

The Route

1. Start from The Bridge Inn, Brewood. The village is on a minor road, signposted off the A449 and the A5, west of Cannock. Centro buses numbers 3 & 12 from Wolverhampton stop here (for information phone 021-200 2700). Considerate roadside parking is available. This route can be linked with Walk 5, which also starts here.

    Go through the white wooden gate opposite The Bridge Inn to join the canal. Walk with the water on your right.

2. After passing under bridge 10, go through the next unnumbered bridge to where the canal widens into a small basin. About 10 yards (9m) beyond this, cross a stile to your left. Turn sharp left to walk with the hedge on your left. Go through a wooden gate and continue. The path enters trees. To your left you will see the balustrades of Avenue Bridge. Cross the bridge and continue along the straight path, through trees.

3. You emerge at a road through a wooden gate. Cross the road and go through the gate opposite. Continue to another gate. Go through and turn right along the road for about 130 yards (120m) to a bridleway on the left. Walk along it, through a gate, towards The Woolley Farm. At the farm, go through a gate and turn right along a track.

4. Turn right at the T-junction and continue to a road. Turn left. Walk

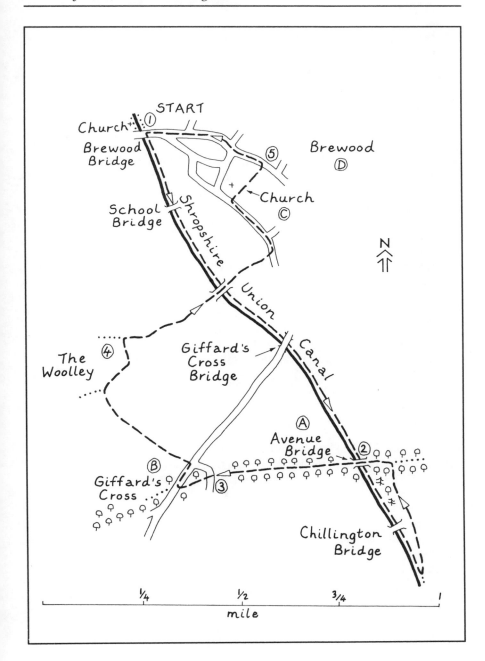

ahead up Dean Street, passing The Admiral Rodney pub, to enter the churchyard by the gate. Turn right to follow the path.

5. Descend steps to the road. Turn left to return to the start.

Places of Interest

A. Avenue Bridge, with its fine stonework and balustrades, is one of the most attractive bridges on the Shropshire Union. Attributed to Telford, it was specially built in 1826 as part of the approaches to Chillington Hall (see B).

B. Giffards Cross, at the entrance to Chillington Hall, marks the spot where, in 1513, Sir John Giffard shot a wild panther with his crossbow. The beast, a gift from an Oriental friend, had escaped, and was about to attack a woman and her child. The Giffard family has held the Chillington estate since about 1180. The present hall dates mainly from the 13th century and is a handsome building with fine interiors. It is the park, however, laid out by Capability Brown in 1770, which is generally considered to be of most interest. It contains many decorative buildings, including the Bowling Green Arch and the Dovecot (built *circa* 1730), a Gothic Temple, an Ionic Temple and a classical bridge over the beautiful lake. The hall and its grounds are open 2.30-5.30pm on Thursdays from May to mid-September, Easter Sunday, and Sundays in August. Admission charge.

C. The Church of St Mary and St Chad, although largely rebuilt in the 16th century, dates originally from the 13th. It is a tall, elegant building containing monuments of the Giffards of Chillington Hall.

D. The village of Brewood (pronounced 'Brood') takes its name from the Celtic 'Bre', which means hill, so giving 'the wood on the hill'. It was once part of the Roman settlement of Pennocrucium, on Watling Street. Today its quiet streets and many attractive Georgian houses make it a rewarding place to explore.

Walk 7:
Penkridge & Pillaton

4.5 miles (7.2km). Moderate

Small scale locks and bridges on the Staffordshire & Worcestershire Canal hark back to a time when goods were transported in virtual silence, and at the pace of a towing horse. The motorway, which is crossed twice on this walk, is a reminder of the price we pay for progress. This walk meanders through the gentle valley of the River Penk.

The Route

1. Penkridge is on the A449 north of Wolverhampton. Turn off this main road through the village centre to park considerately in Haling Road, by The Boat Inn. Numerous buses stop in the village (for information, phone 021-200 2700 or 0785 223344).

   Join the canal by The Boat Inn, and walk with the water on your right. After going underneath the motorway, you leave the canal up steps on the left at Teddesley Park Bridge. Turn right, cross the bridge and turn right again (do not cross the cattle grid).

2. You emerge at a narrow road. Turn left. Go through double wooden gates ahead, at the entrance to Wood Bank Farm. Cross a stile on your right just before a wood, and follow the path over a foot-bridge. Pass another stile and continue. Cross a stile by a broken gate and maintain your direction. Cross two stiles at a little hollow and walk with the fence on your left. In the field corner, ignore the first stile on your left, but cross the one about 30 yards (25m) to the right, and the next, immediately after. Continue ahead.

3. Go through a metal gate in the corner of the field and walk along a track. Go through a second metal gate by a wooden footpath sign, then immediately cross a stile to your left. Go through a gate to emerge at a lane with large houses on your left. Walk along the lane,

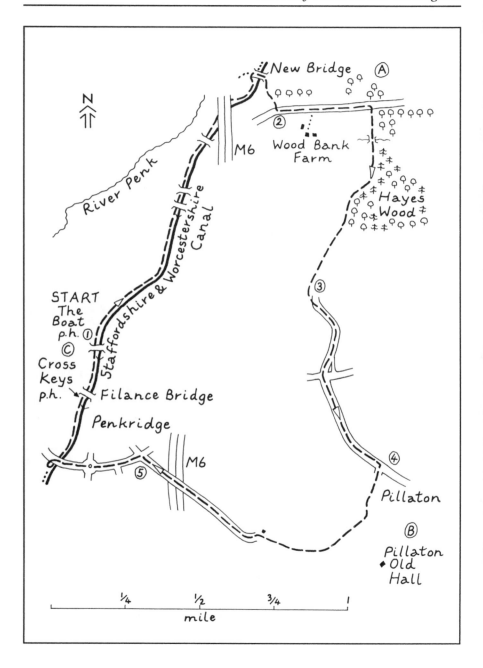

eventually taking the right-hand fork. You come to a road. Cross it and maintain your direction along the road ahead.

4. About 100 yards (90m) after a post box, turn right to walk past Pillaton Hall Farm and Pillaton Old Hall on your left. At a 'Private Property' notice, turn right along a track towards cottages. Go through a gate by the cottages and walk along the road, which crosses the motorway.

5. Turn left at the crossroads and continue. Cross a roundabout. Cross the canal, then immediately descend steps on the left to join the tow-path. Walk with the water on your right to return to the start by Penkridge Lock.

Places of Interest

A. Teddesley Park was once the estate of the Littleton family. The hall, used as a prison camp during the last war, has been demolished.

B. Pillaton Hall was a late 15th-century brick mansion built by the Littleton family. The part which remains standing today contains the gate-house and stone built chapel, although traces of the hall and courtyard can be seen. Visiting is by appointment only, ring 0785 712200. There is a modest charge, which is given to charity.

C. The heart of Penkridge is a busy place, and quite attractive, especially by the canal. The Cross Keys pub at Filance Bridge once stood alone – it has now been swallowed up by new housing, which surrounds the village.

Walk 8:
Brownhills & Chasewater

8 miles (12.9km). Moderate

Over three quarters of this remarkable route consists of waterside walking, and is a fascinating exploration of the northernmost extremity of the Birmingham Canal Navigations. Although this area is quite built up, the canal, as usual, manages to preserve its isolation from the noise and bustle.
It is, in parts, surprisingly rural.

The Route

1. Start from the car park (charge) at the Chase Water Sports Centre and Chasewater Steam Railway, which is signposted off the A5 at Brownhills. There are numerous buses (for information phone 021-200 2700).

   From the car park, walk along the tarmac drive, with Chasewater to the right. Turn left at the station for the Chasewater Steam Railway. Turn right over the bridge across the disused railway, and walk to the road. Turn left.

2. Fork right along Wilkin Road. Turn right at the main road at Brownhills Common, and continue. After the road crosses over the disused railway, turn left at the entrance to Midland Safe Load Indicators. Walk in front of the buildings and continue along the track.

3. You emerge at Pelsall Road Bridge. Turn left along the road for 100 yards (90m), then turn right through a gap in the hedge, to join the canal. Walk with the water on your right.

4. At Pelsall Junction, cross the cast iron bridge and turn left to walk with the canal on your left.

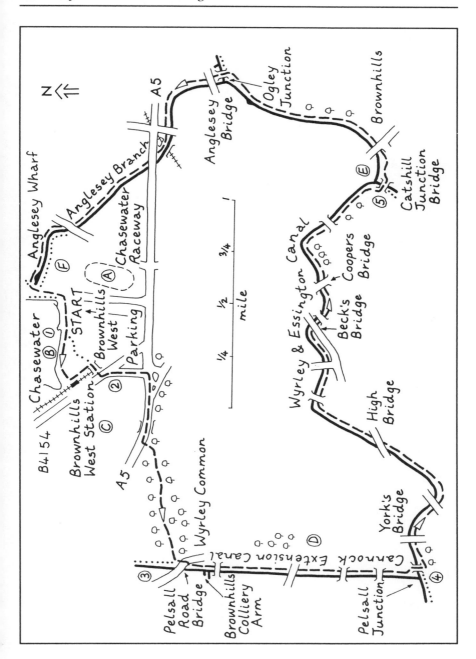

5. At Catshill Junction, cross the bridge and continue with the water on your left. Cross the cast iron bridge over a short canal arm and continue to the very end of the canal. Turn left to walk up the track to return to the start.

Places of Interest

A. This sadly-dilapidated grandstand is part of the old Chasewater Raceway, where trotting races were held as recently as 1984. Its future is uncertain, although demolition seems the most likely possibility.

B. Chasewater was built as a canal feeder reservoir, and was so efficient that at one time its owners, the Wyrley & Essington Canal Company, sold surplus water to other canals. Today it is a popular venue for sailing and water-skiing. Just after it was built, in 1799, the original dam gave way in a spectacular fashion, pouring a torrent of water across Watling Street and into the River Tame near Tamworth. Meadows were left covered in gravel, and some livestock were drowned, but luckily it seems little other damage and no loss of life was caused. The dam was rebuilt, faced with stone, and has held secure ever since. Note the fine octagonal valve house, built in the same style as the once common BCN (Birmingham Canal Navigations) toll houses.

C. Chasewater Steam Railway is based at the old Brownhills West station. The line was part of the Cannock Chase & Wolverhampton Railway, built originally to carry coal from Cannock Chase. Today a splendid collection of nine steam, three diesel and one petrol locomotives are maintained, together with an assortment of historic rolling stock. There is also a museum and a café. Trains run on certain Sundays and Bank Holidays from April to October, with Santa specials at Christmas. Phone 0543 452623 for details.

D. This, the remaining section of the Cannock Extension Canal, was built between 1858 and 1863, and once connected with the Staffordshire & Worcestershire Canal. The old basin here served the Brownhills Collieries. The section north of Watling Street, closed in 1963 due to subsidence, was apparently quite spectacular, with massive embankments and vast brick overflow weirs. It contained over 70 boats, left for scrap, when abandoned.

Brownhills Colliery Basin, on the Cannock Extension Canal

E. At Catshill Junction the Wyrley & Essington Canal splits, with the Daw End branch heading off to the south, and the main line continuing to Ogley Junction. From here it once continued, under an elegant cast iron bridge dated 1829, to Huddlesford Junction, to join the Coventry Canal. This useful link, with its 30 locks, was abandoned in 1954. The Anglesey Branch was built originally as a feeder from Chasewater, but was made navigable in 1850 when the Marquis of Anglesey began coal mining in this area.

F. Coal was loaded into boats at Anglesey Basin until 1967, and the rusting remains of the chutes which were used for this purpose can still be seen. The tow-path remains thick with coal dust. The basin's situation is splendid – overlooked by the dam, it is close to Chasewater Park, and is approached through an important natural landscape.

Bunter Sandstone, which surfaces hereabouts, encourages the growth of unusual heathers and other heathland plants, as well as attracting a wide range of birds. It seems an ideal place for a little restrained development – offering facilities for boaters and secure moorings would bring back some of the vitality the basin must once have had.

Walk 9:
Fazeley Junction &
The Tame Aqueduct

3 miles (4.8km). Easy

A wide variety of interesting features make this a very stimulating short walk. There is some elegant canal architecture at a significant junction, a short nature walk, and an exploration of a massively built aqueduct over the River Tame. The village of Fazeley is easy to find, and has handsome terraces of workers' cottages.

The Route

1. Fazeley is on the A5. Turn off here following the sign for Drayton Manor Park, then take the second left down Brook End for easy parking. Bus no X75 stops close by the junction (for information phone 0785 223344).

   Walk along the main road towards Drayton Manor Park, joining the canal at Coleshill Road Bridge after carefully crossing the road. Walk with the water on your left.

2. Cross the foot-bridge at the canal junction and continue with the water on your right. After the first bridge, turn left down the path signposted 'British Waterways Nature Walk'. Follow this past the first small aqueduct and on to the big aqueduct over the River Tame. Rejoin the tow-path up steps and continue with the canal on your right.

3. Leave the canal at bridge 74, turn right, and walk along the road. Just before houses on your right, turn right along a footpath and cycleway, and follow it past new houses on the right. Emerge at a road, cross it, and continue along the path. Cross a second road and

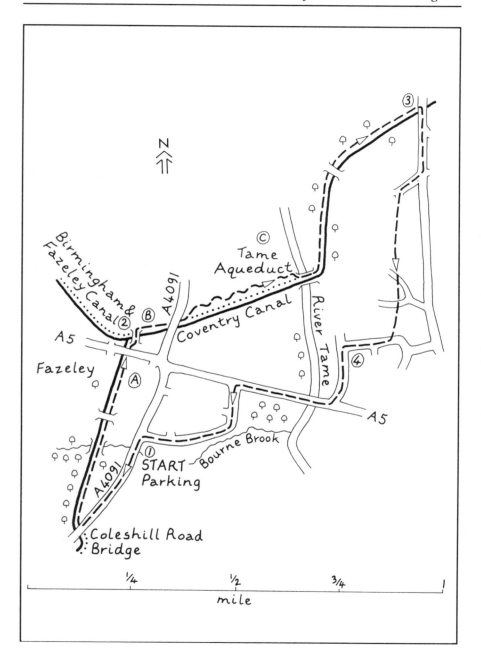

take the path opposite to emerge at a road. Turn right along Parkfield Crescent, which becomes New Street.

4. Turn left at Mount Pleasant. Turn right at the main road, cross Fazeley Bridge, carefully cross the road and continue. Take the first left down Brook End to return to the start.

Fazeley Junction

Places of Interest

A. The original part of this canal-side mill building dates from the late 18th century. It was built by the textile millionaire Peel, who is perhaps best known as the father of Sir Robert Peel (1788-1850), the Conservative statesman who reorganised the London police (hence the nickname 'Bobbies'), and repealed the corn laws following the Irish famine. The family house, long since demolished, was at Drayton Manor, about half a mile (0.8km) to the west. Its old grounds are now occupied by Drayton Manor Park and Zoo.

B. Overlooked by an airy chapel and a large double-fronted red brick canal house, Fazeley Junction marks the end of the original section of the Coventry Canal. This canal was to continue to join the Trent & Mersey Canal at Fradley, but the company had used up all its capital by the time it reached here. The Birmingham & Fazeley Company continued the route westwards to Whittington Brook, and the Trent & Mersey Company completed the line to Fradley from there. This last section was later purchased by the Coventry Canal Company and remains, in name only, as a detached section. Although there are some attractive terraces of workers' cottages in the village, the A5, which roars through, soon makes it apparent that the most satisfactory place to be is beside the canal.

C. This aqueduct crosses the Tame, a river which once had the dubious distinction of being amongst the most polluted in England. It doesn't look too bad now.

Walk 10:
Atherstone & Hartshill

6 miles (9.7km). Moderate

The entry into open countryside from Hartshill is both sudden and surprising, for it is too easy to write this place off as just a suburb of Nuneaton. Its situation, high up on a ridge, makes this a rewarding area in which to walk. All the paths are well marked, and the views are stunning. The return route, along the Coventry Canal, is pleasantly isolated and, at each end, there are canal features of great interest.

The Route

1. Start from the green in front of the Stag & Pheasant pub in Hartshill. There is easy roadside parking, and bus no 48 from Nuneaton (not Sunday, for information phone 0203 559559) stops here. Hartshill is on the B4111, signposted off the A5 at Atherstone. If you come by train to Atherstone, you can join the walk at point 5 by turning right out of the station, and right again at the main road.

    From the green, walk to the right of the Drayton Court estate to the footpath. After a short distance, go through the squeeze stile on the left (ignoring the step stile on the right). Proceed down steps to pass another squeeze stile and continue, ignoring any side paths, and crossing a foot-bridge. At wooden post no 3, turn right.

2. Ignore a waymarked stile on your right, and continue along a fenced path to emerge through a squeeze stile. Walk to your right, towards trees. Enter St Lawrence's Wood along the path. Ignore waymark post no 5, and continue ahead. Turn right at the waymark post and walk around the right-hand side of the field. Go through a gateway and continue with the hedge on your left. At the end of the field, turn right up a track.

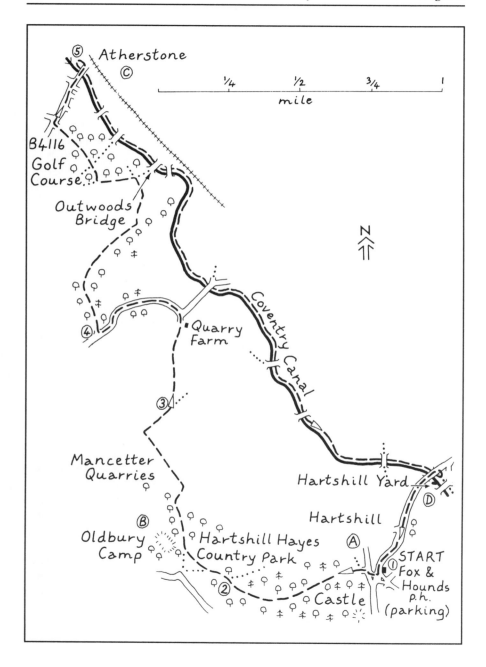

3. Follow the track through a gap in the hedge and continue, to join a road at Quarry Farm. Turn right, then, after about 100 yards (90m) turn left.

4. When the quarry becomes visible on your left, look for a lay-by on the right. Turn right here along a woodland path, crossing four stiles to emerge in a field. Follow the path diagonally to the right, to leave the field at a little bridge over a ditch. Continue along the track to join a lane over a stile, by a gate. Turn left, then turn right at the golf clubhouse. At the main road, turn right.

5. Cross the canal bridge, and turn left to walk down to the water. Visit the top lock, then walk with the canal on your right. You will leave the waterway at bridge 32, but first continue to bridge 31 for a view of Hartshill Yard. Return to the road, turn left, and walk back up the hill to the start.

Places of Interest

A. It was Hugh de Hardreshull, in choosing this site for his castle in 1125, who gave the town its name. From this ridge he could see the distant peaks of Derbyshire on a clear day, and command the surrounding countryside. There is little left to see of his fortification – a motte, some scant remains of a wall, and a trace of what is thought to be the chapel. The Romans before him also recognised the strategic importance of the ridge, and evidence of their occupation – kilns and fragments of pottery – have been unearthed. The poet Michael Drayton (1563-1631) was born in Hartshill. He was a page, at the age of 7, to Sir Henry Goodere (1543-95) who lived nearby at Polesworth. Drayton became a friend of Ben Jonson, and remained a lifelong friend of Goodere. They must have enjoyed some jolly times together in the manor at Polesworth, as Drayton recalls in his Lyrick Pieces:

'They may become John Hewes his lyre
Which off at Polesworth by the fire
Hath made us gravely merry.'

His most notable work was *Polyolbion* (1612-22), a survey of the country, complete with a song for each county. Drayton is buried in Westminster Abbey.

Rothen's Yard at Atherstone

B. Oldbury Camp is a Bronze Age hillfort covering an area of 7 acres. Substantial banks and ditches remain.

C. Atherstone is an attractive 18th-century market town, and those who wish to break the walk here, to explore, will not be disappointed. Hat making is the town's industry, and the factory stands right by the canal. Market Street, Long Street and North Street all have interesting buildings, including the timber-framed Old Swan, which dates from the 16th century. The Church of St Mary, although Victorian, was built on the site of an Austin Friary, which existed in the 14th century. But the town is perhaps best known for its annual game of medieval football, played each Shrove Tuesday, and a relic of games played in Warwickshire and Leicestershire in the 12th century. The match is started by throwing the ball out of the window of the Three Tuns pub – then hundreds of people, following no obvious rules or boundaries, charge around the town. The streets are closed to traffic, and shop windows are boarded up to avoid damage.

The canal basin at Atherstone, at the top of a flight of 11 locks, has a timeless atmosphere, almost removed from 20th century life. At Rothens coal yard you may, if you are lucky, see coal being loaded onto working narrowboats using an old, but well painted, crane. There are usually some other traditional craft moored here, and the lock keeper ensures that the surrounding canalscape is well maintained. It is, in its own understated way, a waterways gem.

D. The British Waterways Maintenance Yard buildings at Hartshill were built in the very finest tradition of English Canal architecture. Arranged around the docks, upon which stand two sturdy cranes, are well proportioned workshops and offices, a dry dock, and an elegant covered wet dock, with neat gables and topped by a clock tower. At the back is a canal manager's house. It is best when viewed from Apple Pie Lane Bridge, number 31.

Walk 11:
The Bratch

4.5 miles (7.2km). Moderate

The Bratch is distinguished by some unusual buildings, and a particularly interesting flight of locks. These are often very busy with boats during the summer cruising season, and are thus a favourite venue for gongoozlers (onlookers). There is an interesting church, and some fine views to enjoy, before the circuit is completed along the tow-path beside the Staffs & Worcs Canal.

The Route

1. If you are coming by car, start from The Bratch Picnic site. Turn off the A449 at its junction with the A463, taking the minor road signposted to Trysull, Seisdon, Lower Penn and Wombourne. Fork left along Bratch Lane to find the car park (open 8am – 9pm) on the left just before the canal bridge. Those arriving by bus should join the canal at Wombourne (for information phone 021-200 2700).

    Cross over the bridge from the picnic site and walk up to the octagonal toll house. Continue with the canal on your left.

2. Go under Awbridge Bridge and leave the canal by turning right up to the road. Cross the bridge and continue ahead. When the road bends to the left, go ahead through a gateway, following a waymark. Walk to the left of the electricity pylon to descend to the road. Turn right through a gap in the hedge and walk into Trysull. Turn left by the church.

3. Turn left down the waymarked path immediately after the Vicarage. Cross a stile and walk diagonally to the right, aiming for the electricity pylon furthest to the right. You descend from the brow of the field to a stile by a gate in the far corner. Cross it and turn left. After 70 yards (65m) turn right down the waymarked drive to Woodford Grange.

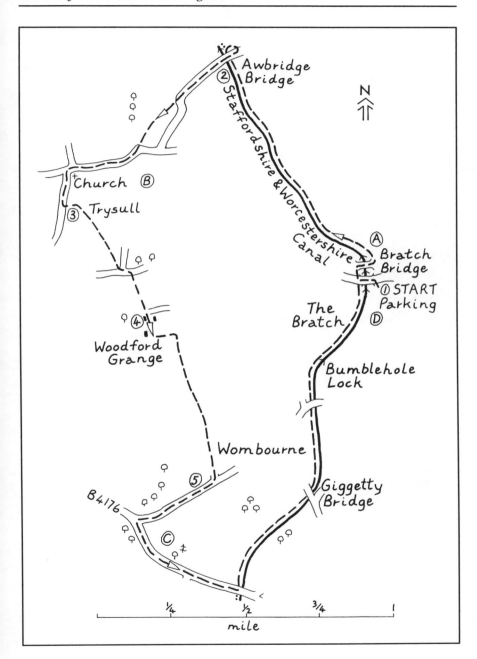

4. Walk to the left of the buildings, go through a gap in a fence and turn left to cross a field. At the edge, turn right to walk with the hedge on your left. When the hedge curves to the left, maintain your direction to join a track which comes in from the right. Continue ahead to the main road.

5. Turn right and walk along Millfields to the next junction, where you turn left. Reach the canal just before the Wagon & Horses pub. Turn left down to the tow-path and walk with the canal on your right, back to The Bratch.

Places of Interest

A. The three locks at The Bratch are overlooked by a tall octagonal toll house and a sloping brick bridge – an attractive architectural unit and an excellent viewpoint from which to ponder the workings of this flight. At first sight, the lock chambers seem impossibly close together, with no intervening lengths of canal, or pounds, from which to fill, or into which to empty, each adjacent lock. But a closer study reveals culverts under the tow-path, connected to ponds on the other side of the hedge. As a boat goes either up or down, water will be seen pouring in, or out, of these.

B. All Saints Church, Trysull, still contains a Norman archway and some very early windows, although the tower is medieval. Two stained-glass figures in the east window date from the 14th century.

C. Hidden amongst the undergrowth are the remains of rock houses (see Walk 20).

D. This extravagant Art Nouveau style building is a waterworks, built in 1895.

Walk 12:
The Black Country Museum

2.5 miles (4km). Easy

A visit to The Black Country Museum should be high on everyone's itinerary when in this area. Years of painstaking work have established a worthy monument to the life and work of the people of the West Midlands. Combined with a short canal-side walk and a chance to feed the ducks in Victoria Park, it is a splendid way to spend a day.

The Route

1. Start from The Black Country Museum. This is well signposted in Tipton Road (A4037) in Dudley. Many buses stop here (021-200 2700 for details).

   From the museum, walk to the left along Tipton Road. Turn right at the traffic lights, then take the first left into Baker Street. Turn left at the grocer's shop, cross the canal, and join the tow-path. Walk with the water on your left. When the tow-path joins Elliot Road and Beehive Walk, continue with the water to your left.

2. Cross the foot-bridge at Factory Junction and now walk with the water on your right, towards the locks. At the bottom lock, cross the black and white iron foot-bridge, to maintain your direction, now with the canal to your left.

3. You pass Caggy Stevens boatyard on the opposite bank, marked by two tow-path bridges (one dated BCN 1880) and moored boats. Continue under the foot-bridge, then under a pipe bridge, to leave the canal at the next bridge, opposite the railway signal box. Walk down Watery Lane. Cross Queens Road to enter Victoria Park.

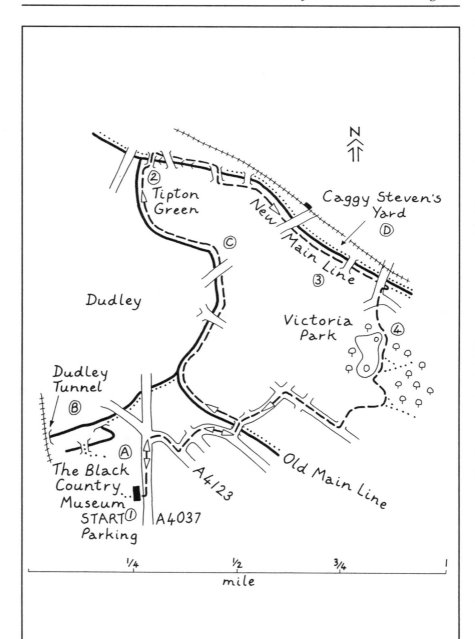

4. Walk around the left-hand side of the lake. Follow the path to the left of the tennis courts, then fork right to pass houses on your left. Leave the park and turn right along Park Lane West. Take the second left into Baker Street. Cross the canal foot-bridge and turn right. Turn right at the main road, then left at the traffic lights to return to the start.

Sturdy canal fixtures at Factory Locks

Places of Interest

A. The Staffordshire Thick Coal Seam, 30 feet (9m) in depth, lies just below the surface in this area. Its extraction, the industry it supported, and the dereliction, dirt and smoke it caused gave rise to the name 'The Black Country'. Such small scale mining is no longer economic, and the manufacturing industry which remains to remind us of those times is now, thankfully, much cleaner. This museum, established in 1975 on a 26 acre site, seeks to collect, preserve, research and display items relevant to the area's social and industrial history. To this end a complete small canal-side village has been built, using relocated buildings from all over the area, which would otherwise have been demolished. There is a pub where you can have a pint of local ale, a sweet shop, a chapel, a grocers, a hardware store, numerous original houses and a small iron works. Within the site you may visit a coal mine, ride a cakewalk at the fairground, or travel on a trolley bus or a tram. Superb examples of working narrowboats are moored in the canal arm, and chain making, nail making and boat building is carried out in the workshops around The Boatdock. Open daily. Admission charge. Café and shop.

The Black Country Museum

B. Dudley Tunnel was completed in 1792, and is one of the wonders of the waterways. It connects with a complex network of underground caverns, basins and mines, including the 'Singing Cavern', reached via a new tunnel, built in 1989. Although 3154 yards (2884m) long from end to end, the total amount of tunnelling exceeds 5000 yards (4572m). Closed to through traffic for many years, it finally reopened in 1992, albeit with restrictions. The Dudley Canal Trust runs boat trips into the tunnel from The Black Country Museum.

C. The Fountain pub was once the headquarters of William Perry, a prizefighter known as the 'Tipton Slasher'. A canal boatman, he became champion in 1850, and held the title for seven years.

D. Still known as Watery Lane Junction, this was where the Tipton Green and Toll End Communication crossed the main line, from 1809-1960. Caggy Stevens boatyard now occupies all that remains.

Walk 13:
Netherton Tunnel

4.5 miles (7.2km). Moderate — you must bring a torch

This is a safe, but very exciting, walk deep underground through one of the longest canal tunnels open to navigation. The outward journey, over the top, offers sweeping views across the Severn Valley to the hills beyond. This route can be linked with Walk 14.

The Route

1. Start from the car park in the park opposite The Wonder pub. This is on Dudley Road West, which is the A457. The entrance is marked by four prominent red metal triangles. Bus no 87 from central Birmingham stops here.

   From the car park, walk along the path, with the allotments to your right. You emerge at a busy main road. Cross it and turn right. After about 200 yards (185m) turn left up a path with a railing, to join a cul-de-sac. Turn right, then take the first left. Turn right at the next junction into Birch Crescent. Turn right at the crossroads.

2. Turn left by the Post Office and continue. Turn right up Barncroft Road, and after about 50 yards (45m), take the path on your right, up steps. You emerge from Pendennis Drive and turn left up the hill. At the end of Red Lion Close turn right up Regent Road. Turn left at Oakham Road and continue.

3. Turn right at the public footpath sign after Warrens Hall Nursing Home. Follow the lane, ignoring a stile on your left just after Netherton Hall Stables. When the tarmac ends, continue ahead along a path.

4. At a cross-paths with a public footpath sign, turn right to walk downhill towards the left-hand side of the pond. Pass the pond along

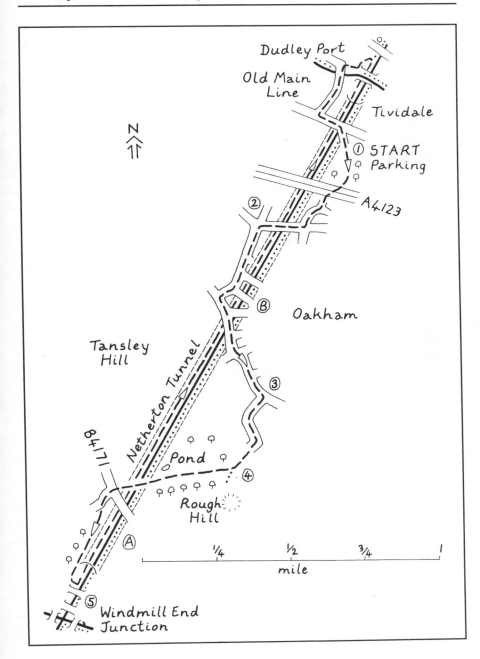

the main path, to join a road. Cross it and continue down the road opposite for about 100 yards (95m), then veer off left along the path towards the prominent engine house chimney, passing football pitches on your right.

5. Walk 14 can be joined at this point. Go down to the canal and turn left to walk through the tunnel, using a torch. You emerge from the tunnel, walk under an aqueduct and turn sharp left up a track by the tunnel keeper's house. Join the higher canal and turn right. Climb up steps at the first bridge and turn left along the road. At the main road turn left to return to the start.

Places of Interest

A. This circular brick structure is one the tunnel's seven ventilation shafts.

B. You are now half way through the 3027 yards (2768m) long Netherton Tunnel, deep underground and yet 453 feet (138m) above sea level. The last major canal tunnel to be built in Britain, it opened in 1858. Lit originally by gas, and then later by electricity, it is 17 feet (5.2m) wide at water level. With twin tow-paths, it was, at that time, a very modern concept.

Walk 14:
Windmill End

3 miles (4.8km). Easy

From the church on Netherton Hill, where this walk starts, it is possible to enjoy a vast panorama of the West Midlands, over Brierly Hill, Dudley and Stourbridge to the valley of the River Stour, Kinver Edge (see Walk 21) and on into Herefordshire. The waterside component is, as usual, more intimate, and quite fascinating.

The Route

1. Start from the church on the summit of Netherton Hill, between the A4036 and A459, where Highbridge Road, Hill Street and Church Road meet, near Dudley. There is easy roadside parking, and bus numbers 9, 282, 283 & 285 stop here (for information phone 021-200 2700).

   Walk down Church Road. Turn left at Castleton Street. Cross the road carefully and continue, looking for the conspicuous red-brick Netherton Arts Centre on the right. Go along the path to the left of the Arts Centre, and maintain your direction down shallow steps to join the main avenue through Netherton Park. Turn right.

2. You emerge at Lynbrook Close. Go to the right to join the main road, where you turn left. After about 100 yards (90m), go down a lane on the right, beside an old garage, and marked with grey metal railings. When the path divides, walk to the left towards the old engine house.

3. You can join Walk 13 here. Cross the canal bridge and turn right, going over the red-brick bridge at the junction and continuing with the water on your right.

4. Leave the canal through the sailing club car park (look for the masts)

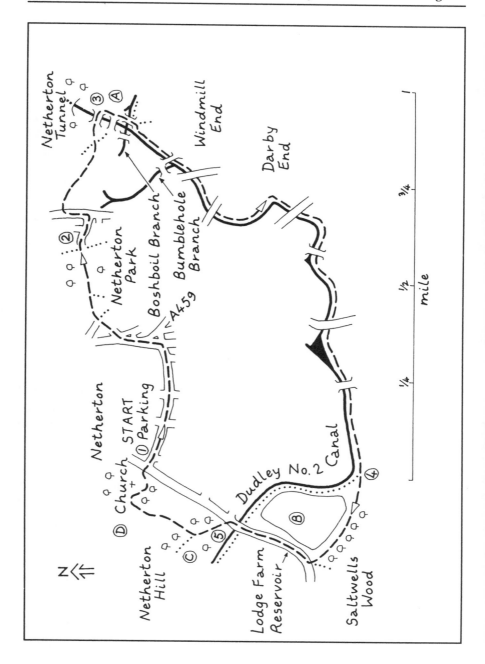

and walk with the reservoir on your right. Turn right at the road and continue, crossing the canal, which is in a deep cutting.

5. Enter Saltwells Wood Nature Reserve over a stile on the left, and walk along the path. Go through a squeeze stile and turn right, following the wooden fence. Veer left to walk beside the cricket pitch up to the church. Enter the churchyard through a wide gap in the railings and return to the start.

Places of Interest

A. Overlooked by Cobb's Engine House, which once worked to drain local mines, the area around Windmill End Junction provides plenty of canal interest. Netherton Tunnel, which branches away to the north here, was a later addition to the Dudley No 2 Canal. The two branches to the south of the junction – the quaintly named Boshboil and Bumblehole Arms – once formed a loop on the canal's original course. They were by-passed by the present straight section of canal when the tunnel was built. Nail making, anchor and chain making and mining were all once important industries in Netherton, but, as is common in Britain, most of these have now disappeared.

B. Lodge Farm Reservoir was built in 1838, and covers part of the old line of the canal. The new, more direct, line was instigated by Thomas Brewin, who built a new tunnel. Although still known as 'Brewin's Tunnel', it was 'opened' in 1858, and is crossed later on during this walk. The reservoir stores water for the canal, and is used for sailing and fishing.

C. Saltwell's Wood is a local nature reserve, taking its name from a salt spa which existed hereabouts in the 17th century.

D. St Andrew's Church, on Netherton Hill, was built 1827-30 and is unremarkable save for its splendid position. The views from the churchyard, which apparently contains the mass graves of plague victims, are excellent.

Walk 15:
The Galton Valley

4.5 miles (7.2km). Easy

It is easy canal-side walking all the way on this route, which explores the two levels of the Birmingham Main Line in the Galton Valley Canal Park. The deep cuttings, now overgrown with small trees, blackberry bushes and banks of rosebay willow herb, are colourful in summer, and attract much wildlife.

The Route

1. From the A457 in Smethwick, turn off for Rolfe Street station, which is very close to the start of this walk. Bus numbers 445, 450, 450A, 460 & 628 stop here (for information phone 021-200 2700). Go down North Western road, opposite the station, to the start at the canal bridge. You can park in Gt Arthur Street, close by.

    Go down steps to join the high level canal, and walk with the water on your right, eventually going through Summit Tunnel. The canal goes under the motorway for a while. Shortly after it emerges, you cross a brick built canal bridge, and continue with the water on your left, descending three locks.

2. Cross the iron foot-bridge at the bottom lock, and walk with the canal on your right, following the sign 'Birmingham 4.5 miles'.

3. When the Old Main Line canal joins from the left at Smethwick Junction, turn sharp left to keep the water on your right. Walk up the locks. Make a short diversion to explore the Engine Branch, crossing the aqueduct on the left, and going as far as the first bridge. Rejoin the Old Main Line to return to the start, climbing up the ramp at the bridge by Smethwick New Pumping Station.

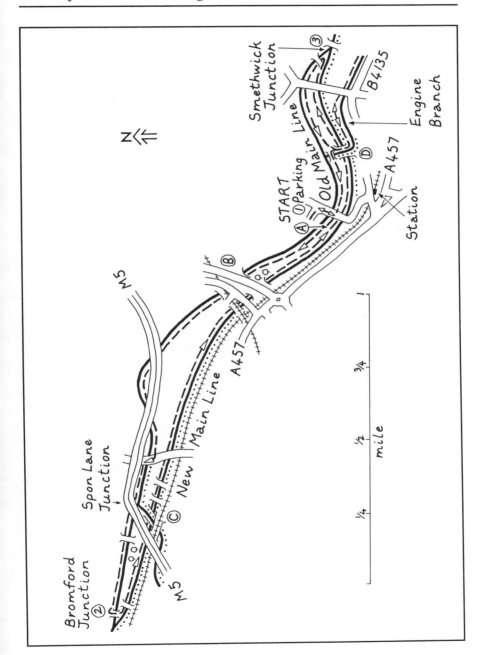

Places of Interest

A. Smethwick New Pumping Station was built in the late 19th century to raise water from the Birmingham level up to the Wolverhampton level.

B. Summit Tunnel, and Galton Tunnel on the lower level, were built in 1974 when Telford Way was constructed. Rather charmless concrete tubes, it is interesting to compare them with earlier tunnels visited on these walks: Cookley, for example, on Walk 21.

C. Just after the M5 motorway crosses, the 473 feet (144m) level, or Old Main Line, crosses on Stewart Aqueduct, heading towards Oldbury Junction, which is visited on Walk 16.

This elegant cast-iron structure, the Telford Aqueduct, carries the Engine Branch over the New Main Line.

D. Telford Aqueduct, which carries the Engine Branch over the lower, 453 feet (138m) level, is a very elegant structure, tastefully painted in grey, white and red. The canal is contained within in a trough, beside which the tow-path is supported by no less than 22 small arches. Both are carried by a fine sweep of open work cast-iron supports. Walking over the aqueduct, the Engine Branch is worth exploring as far as the first bridge. Built as a feeder from Rotton Park Reservoir, the 'engine' was a James Watt pumping engine, now in the Museum of Science and Industry (see Walk 17).

Walk 16:
Titford Pools

2.8 miles (4.5km). Easy

In the midst of this heavily built-up area, and straddled by the motorway, the Titford Pools remain an oasis of peace and a valuable resource for wildlife. This easy walk, which visits them, also includes a short length of canal with a fascinating industrial history.

The Route

1. This walk starts from the Holts Brewery Inn (New Inn), which is on the B4182 in Oldbury. Bus no 120 from Birmingham city centre stops here (for information phone 021-200 2700). Langley Green Station is close by. You can park in Underhill Street, by the pub.

   Join the canal opposite the pub and walk with the water on your right.

2. Cross the concrete foot-bridge at the junction (underneath the motorway), then turn sharp right to walk with the canal now on your left, towards Wolverhampton. After passing Seven Stars Bridge and a boatbuilder's yard, you leave the canal at the next bridge, and turn left along the road. Cross carefully to the other side and continue.

3. Carefully cross Wolverhampton Road at the roundabout, and then two estate roads, to take the road between Halfords' Superstore and Toys 'r Us.

4. Carefully cross the road to join the canal by the electricity pylon. Walk beside Titford Pools with the water on your right. Look out for the Holts Brewery Inn (New Inn), where you started.

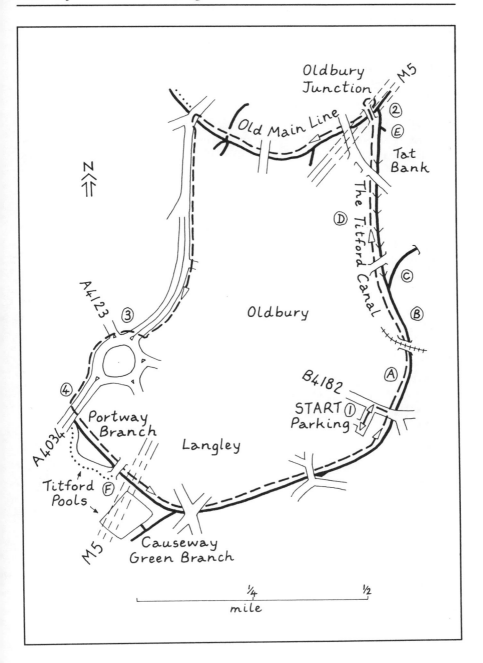

Places of Interest

A. You join the Titford Canal on the highest pound still navigable on the Birmingham Canal Navigations – fully 511 feet (156m) above sea level.

B. These imposing red-brick buildings are the Langley Maltings. Once known as Showells Maltings, they were built during the 1890s, and are used these days by the Wolverhampton & Dudley Breweries, brewers of Banks's beers.

C. The Tat Bank Branch joins the canal just above the top lock, by the pump house. It is a feeder from Rotton Park Reservoir. The first half a mile (0.8km) or so was made navigable in the 1860s , but was closed to traffic by the turn of the century. The pump house still operates, although modern pumps have replaced the original beam engine.

D. Between the third and fourth locks down in the Oldbury flight a hump in the tow-path is all that remains of the Jim Crow Branch. This once served the alkali and phosphorous works of Jim Crow, a local benefactor. Oldbury Locks are also known as 'The Crow'.

E. This basin is the only surviving part of the arm which served Springfield's Midland Tar Distillery. Between 1889 and 1966 it was the base of a fleet of 'gas' boats owned by Thomas Clayton, a name which became synonymous with the BCN. Each boat carried 20 tons of crude tar, from local gasworks, in covered holds.

F. Titford Pools, a canal supply reservoir, occupies the 'V' between the truncated arms of two canal branches: The Portway Branch, and the Causeway Green Branch. Here ducks and waterfowl swim, oblivious of the motorway, high above.

Walk 17:
Gas Street Basin &
Farmer's Bridge

2 miles (3.2km). Easy

In the very heart of Birmingham there exists a quieter, almost subterranean, world, isolated from the rush and traffic of the surrounding streets. Down by the canal it is still possible, in places, to imagine life and work during the 19th century, when these waterways played such a vital role in the Industrial Revolution.

The Route

1. In Central Birmingham, follow signs for the International Convention Centre and National Indoor Arena. Park (charge) in Holliday Street by the Holiday Inn Hotel, off Suffolk Street Queensway (A4400), near Paradise Circus. New Street Station is close by, along Navigation Street. There are many buses (for information phone 021-200 2700).

   Walk along Holliday Street, and turn right into Bridge Street. Immediately after passing The James Brindley pub on your left, join the canal at Gas Street Basin. Walk with the water on your left.

2. Cross the foot-bridge at Farmers Bridge Junction, to face the National Indoor Arena. Turn right to walk down the locks with the water on your right.

3. After passing the bottom lock, go under Snow Hill Bridge and look for a doorway on your left, where the tow-path is slightly raised. Walk up to the main road (Old Snow Hill) and turn left.

   Follow signs to St Chad's Cathedral, going through an underpass. Pass the cathedral on your left and take the underpass signposted to the Central Shopping Area. Emerge and keep following the signs. At

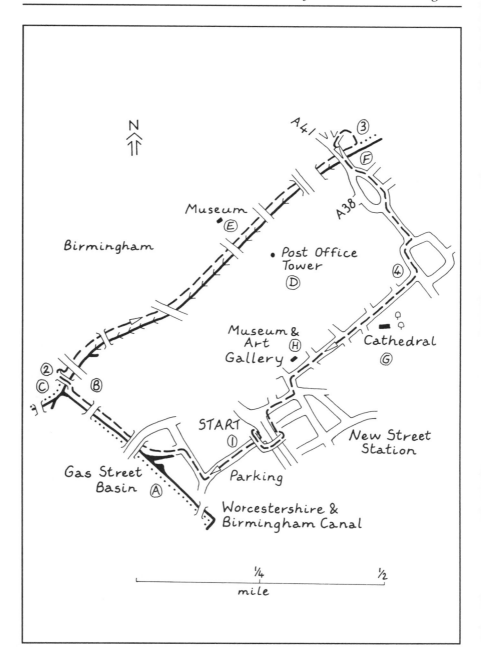

Colmore Circus you face a building called The Wesleyan. Go down the underpass and turn right, still following signs for The Central Shopping Area.

4. Turn right and walk along Colmore Row, passing the Council Offices and coming to the Town Hall, with its neo-classical columns. Turn left and cross the road at the traffic lights. Walk down Paradise Street and turn left at the end. Cross the foot-bridge at Brunel Street to return to Holliday Street.

Places of Interest

A. The Worcester & Birmingham Canal joins the Birmingham Canal at Gas Street Basin. The central 'causeway' used to extend the whole way across, and was known as 'The Worcester Bar'. The Birmingham Canal would not allow the Worcester & Birmingham Canal to actually join it for fear of losing water, so all goods had to be transhipped across the bar. Once hemmed in by tall warehouses and lit by gas lights, Gas Street had a very special atmosphere. This has now been lost to the developers. There are, however, always interesting traditional craft moored here.

B. The International Convention Centre opened in 1991. It can house meetings for up to 3000 people.

C. The National Indoor Arena is the setting for athletics, conventions or concerts. It can seat up to 13,000 people.

D. The Telecom Tower is 498 feet (152m) tall. It came into use in 1966.

E. The Museum of Science and Industry contains the world's oldest working steam engine, together with a vast collection of other industrial relics, cars, motor-cycles and aircraft.

F. The Roman Catholic Cathedral of St Chad was built between 1839-41 by A W N Pugin, in what used to be the gunmaker's quarter. Today it stands bemused in the midst of overpasses, underpasses, tall tower blocks and deep subways. There is the distinct impression that someone would have liked to have knocked it down to make room for a road, but wouldn't dare...

G. The Anglican Cathedral of St Philip was designed by Thomas Archer, and completed in 1725. Built in the Palladian style, it has somehow managed to retain a little open space around it.

H. The Museum and Art Gallery, the imposing Town Hall, and the Central Library, with its vast Shakespeare Collection, enclose Chamberlain Square.

Walk 18:
The Aston Ring

5.5 miles (8.8km). Easy

A long walk wholly beside the canal. From the brightly painted modern buildings of the Aston Science park, to the old wharfs and loading bays at Digbeth (a reminder of the canal's original purpose), there is always plenty of interest.

The Route

1. Start from The Aston Science Park, which is well signposted off the A4540 (Dartmouth Middleway) at Lister Street, and is right by the campus of The University of Birmingham. There is plenty of roadside parking in Holt Street and around the University. Many buses serve the University and Science Park (for information phone 021-200 2700).

    Walk back to Dartmouth Middleway along Lister Street, which crosses Holt Street, and turn right passing the modern steel and glass offices of Quest Vitamins. Look on your right for a walkway between the offices to the canal. Turn right and walk with the water on your left.

2. Turn right at Aston Junction, by the lock, and continue with the canal on your left.

3. You approach Salford Junction over an aqueduct, with the motorway above. Turn right and stay on the tow-path. Do not cross the cast iron foot-bridge numbered 110, but walk underneath it. With the water still on your left, follow the blue sign towards Warwick.

4. Turn right by the elegant cast iron foot-bridge at Bordesley Junction, keeping the canal on your left. You pass Digbeth Basin and climb the five Ashted Locks before walking through Ashted Tunnel. Pass Ashted Top Lock and walk under Heneage Street Bridge. Look on the

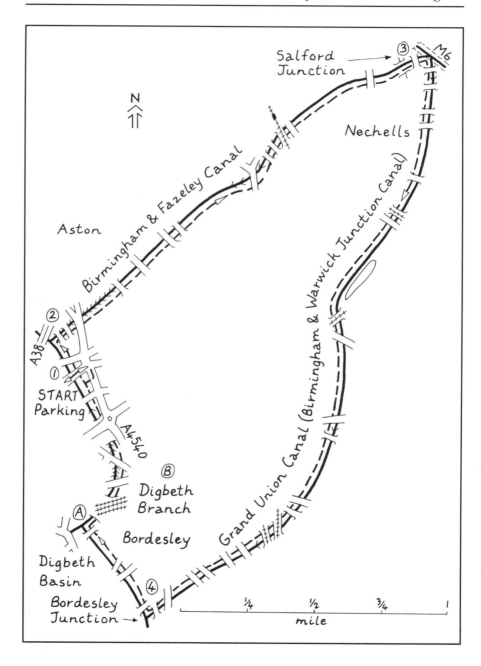

right for the path which leaves the canal, between blue posts. Turn left at the main road, and left at Lister Street to return to the start.

Places of Interest

A. This is The Birmingham Gun-Barrel Proof House. It has a charming frontage in Banbury Street, and was built in 1813.

B. The Digbeth Branch probably opened before 1799. It has six locks, and a tunnel 103 yards (94m) long, crammed into its modest length.

A working boat on the Birmingham & Fazeley Canal

Walk 19:
Stourbridge & Delph

5 miles (8km). Moderate

*The Redhouse Cone marks the start of this exploration of Black County Canals.
The Stourbridge 16 and Delph flights of locks are both impressive and visually
exciting. The hills they climb offer sweeping views over an area no longer
darkened by the smoke of industry.*

The Route

1. Start from the Red House Cone Museum, which is a prominent landmark on the A491 in Amblecote, near Stourbridge. There is roadside parking in Bridge Street, and the museum has a car park. Numerous buses stop here (details from 021-200 2700).

   Walk out of Bridge Street, turn right along the main road, cross the canal and walk down to the tow-path on your left. Walk with the water on your right. At Stourbridge Top Lock, cross the canal and continue with the water on your left.

2. The tow-path crosses an iron foot-bridge. Go up the steps ahead to a road, and turn left. Cross the canal and turn left up The Promenade. At a T-junction turn left along Hill Street. Turn right along Delph Road. Continue ahead along Brettell Lane, crossing the road at the zebra crossing. Fork right down Bull Street.

3. Fork left at the Bull's Head pub, cross the canal and continue ahead along a footpath. Emerge at a road through a squeeze stile. Go ahead to a T-junction, where you walk straight ahead along a path to the left of The General Stores. Go through another squeeze stile and continue ahead. You come to a fence with shallow steps up to the left. Go up the steps, then walk to the right, with a fence on your right. Join a road through a gate. Turn left, and left again, to walk 50 yards (45m) along the road to the canal on your right.

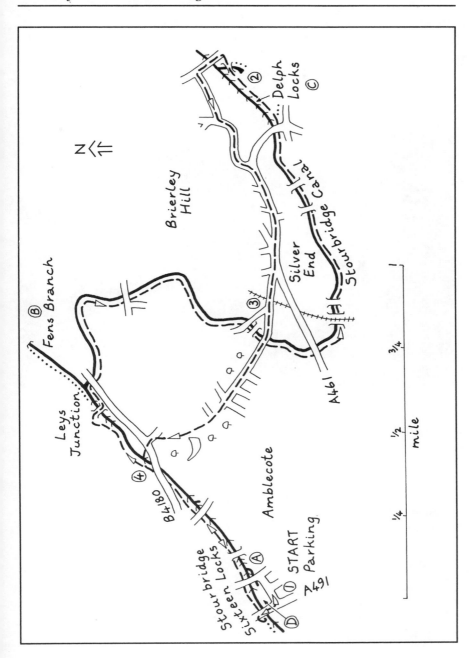

4. Carefully cross the canal at the lock, and walk with the water on your left, back to the Red House Cone Museum.

Canalside architecture alongside the Stourbridge 16

Places of Interest

A. Look out for the handsome timber warehouse known as 'Dadford's shed', above lock 12. There were once many similar buildings on the waterways network, but most have been demolished. This one will soon need restoration.

Locks 11 and 10 are known as 'The staircase', although they are not actually arranged that way (the top gates of one lock are also the bottom gates of the next in a true 'staircase'). Look out also for the handsome terraces of cottages, the dock, and the diminutive iron split bridges.

B. The Fens Branch feeds clear water into the canal from the Pensnett Reservoir, or Fens Pools.

C. Delph Locks are known also as 'The Nine Locks', but if you count them, you will find only eight! Remains of the original flight of nine can be seen beside the present locks, rebuilt in 1850. The overflow weirs beside them are spectacular after rainy weather.

D. Taking advantage of the new canal, local industrialist Richard Bradley built the Red House Cone in 1790. It is 90 feet (27m) tall. Originally producing window glass, production then switched to bottles, to be followed by tableware and engraved crystal. It has been owned since 1881 by Stuart & Sons. Open Monday-Friday. Admission charge.

Walk 20:
Kinver

7.2 miles (11.6km). Strenuous

Kinver is a well-known West Midlands beauty spot, with very attractive countryside and some fascinating historical and geological features. The Staffordshire & Worcestershire Canal, which is followed on the second part of this walk, accompanies the River Stour in an intimate valley and this, combined with the mellow red brick buildings associated with the canal, completes the circuit in a particularly charming way.

The Route

1. Start from any of the three free car parks off the High Street in Kinver, a village beside the A449 near Kidderminster. Bus numbers 242 from Stourbridge and 582 from Wolverhampton (Saturday only) stop in the village (for information phone 021-200 2700).

   Walk along the High Street, passing the Post Office and Ye Olde White Harte Hotel on your left, and turn left up Stone Lane. After about 0.5 mile (0.8km) a road comes in from the right, and trees appear on your left. Take the path into the trees for 100 yards (95m) and look for a National Trust sign on your left at a cross-paths. Walk past the sign to explore the rock houses, then return to the cross-paths and walk ahead, ignoring shallow steps up to your left. After 100 yards (95m) you reach a clearing.

2. Follow the clear gravel path uphill to your left, through woods. At a cross-paths, turn left. When the path forks, keep to the right. You come to a viewpoint, descend down sandstone steps, then gradually climb again. After passing rock houses on your left you come to a squeeze stile. Go through and turn left up a steep track, following the Worcestershire Way waymark.

3. At a clearing with picnic tables and an information board, turn right

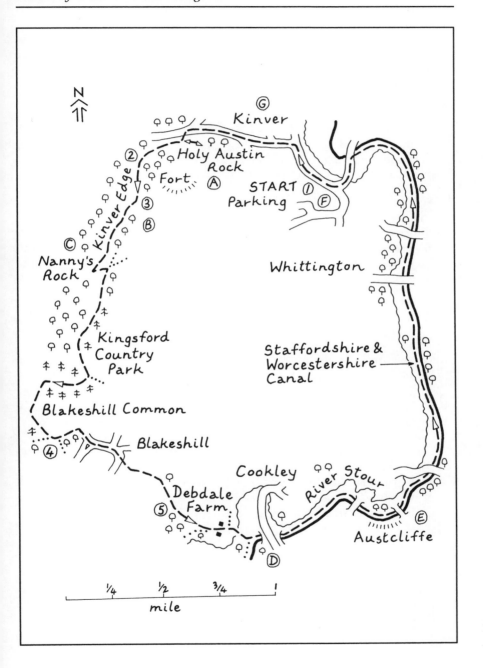

following the Worcestershire Way. When the path forks, go to the right. Turn right at the next junction, by a post with blue waymarks. Again the path forks by a waymark post. Take the left fork. Turn left at a path T-junction and follow the red marks on the trees.

4. You emerge at a T-junction with a wide track. Turn left and continue ahead, ignoring a footpath off to the right. You join a narrow road. Continue ahead. Turn right at a T-junction with the main road and continue. Where the road bends to the right look for the gate and public footpath sign to Cookley on the left. Follow this path.

5. You come to a stile. Cross it and look for another stile ahead. Cross it and walk along the floor of a little valley. Pass a pond on your left, climb a step stile by a gate and walk to the left of the farm buildings. Take a track to your right to cross a bridge over the River Stour. Continue ahead to join the canal. Walk with the water on your right. At Kinver Lock turn left along Mill Lane, to return to the start.

Places of Interest

A. There are excellent examples of dwellings known as rock houses, carved out of Triassic sandstone, at Holy Austin Rock. Rooms, windows, doorways, chimneys and remarkably slim walls can all be seen. In some rooms there are even cupboards carved in the rock. A few were occupied until 1950, and there was a café here until 1967.

The rock houses were quite comfortable. Walls were plastered, fireplaces built, and pictures hung. With tiles on the floor they appeared, from the inside at least, just like a normal house – apart from a lack of windows in all except the front room. Rock dwellings were recorded here in a book published in 1777, and it is likely that caves were occupied earlier than that. The name, Holy Austin, may hark back to a time when an Augustine Friar lived here.

During the 19th century, when the nearby Hyde Iron Works was in full production, there was a great demand for accommodation in this area, and 12 families were living here in 1851. One of these, the Shaws, were in continuous occupation for over 150 years, until 1935.

The historian, folklorist and novelist Sabine Baring-Gould (1834-1924) made Holy Austin Rock the setting for his book *Bladys of the Stewponey*. This was made into a film and shot on location here in 1919.

Take care when exploring the rock houses, which are on several levels and have become slippery over the years.

B. Kinver Edge consists of a spectacular ridge amidst 200 acres of heath and woodland, given to the National Trust in 1917. Popular with day-trippers from the West Midlands, it can become quite busy on fine Sundays in summer.

C. The caves at Nanny's Rock are far less sophisticated than those at Holy Austin, and more isolated. Also known as 'Meg-o-Fox-hole', they are known to have been occupied until 1617 by Margaret of the fox earth, who is recorded in the parish register. The 'nanny' referred to is thought to have lived here as a recluse in the late 19th century. She made herbal potions, although apparently few people had the courage to come and buy them.

D. Cookley tunnel is 65 yards (59m) long, rough hewn from the living rock. It has a tow-path through it. This is unusual, considering its age (the canal was opened in 1772), but probably reflects the ease with which the local sandstone can be worked. Part of the village of Cookley sits astride the canal, above the tunnel.

E. Until very recently the cliffs at Austcliffe actually overhung the canal. Deemed to be a hazard, they were trimmed back by British Waterways.

F. The Church of St Peter stands 150 feet (46m) above the village, overlooking the valley of the River Stour. The present building dates from the 14th and 15th century, although its origins are certainly much earlier. Inside there is a very fine brass of Sir Edward Grey (died 1528), with his wife and children, and a copy of the Charter granted by Ethelbad in 736, granting '10 cessapis of land to my general Cyniberte for a religious house'.

G. Kinver Edge was recognised for its strategic value during the Iron Age, and a promontory fort was built. The Romans came and went, and then the fort was probably occupied by Wulthere, King of

Mercia, during the 5th century. The first record of the village, in the form of a charter granted by Ethelbad, dates from 736. It was later recorded as 'Chenevare' in the Domesday survey, when a few cottages were standing on the high ground near the church, above the flood level of the river. A great forest stood in this area, with the timber being used for iron smelting. The clearings thus formed grazed sheep, providing food and a local wool industry. Water from the River Stour powered the fulling (cloth) mills until 1830, when Kidderminster became the centre of this trade. Kinver then thrived when Hyde Mill, the local iron works, had its short heyday, but closures around 1870 brought a mass depopulation. After a period in the wilderness, the Kinver Light Railway, known as the 'Kinver Tram', made access from the West Midlands easy, and the village's fate was sealed. It became, and still is, part resort and part dormitory for the Black Country.

Walk 21:
Bewdley & Ribbesford

3.8 miles (6.1km). Strenuous

A gentle stroll along the bank of the River Severn is followed by a fairly stiff climb through the woods above Ribbesford to enjoy some fine views over the river valley. The return journey includes a visit to an exceptionally beautiful church, and the opportunity to explore Bewdley, a charming Georgian river port.

The Route

1. Bewdley is just off the A456, about 3 miles (4.8km) from Kidderminster, and is served by many buses (for information phone 0345 212555), and the Severn Valley Railway Company from Kidderminster station (for information phone 0299 403816). The riverside pay & display car park is clearly signposted from Bewdley Bridge.

   Walk along the riverside path from the bridge, with the water on your left. Shortly after passing under a bridge, you join a riverside road. Continue. About 150 yards (135m) after the road leaves the riverside, walk up a path to the right of The Woodman pub.

2. You climb past a broken wooden gate, then join a track. Turn sharp right for 45 yards (40m), then take a clear path uphill on your left. Follow this clear path over a cross-paths, until you reach two wooden farm sheds on your left.

3. Look for a waymark post for the Worcestershire Way on your right, and follow this path down to a stile. Cross it and walk with a hedge on your left. Cross another stile and continue down the narrow path. Cross another stile and walk towards the church at Ribbesford. Cross a stile, enter the churchyard and visit the church. The entrance porch is to the left.

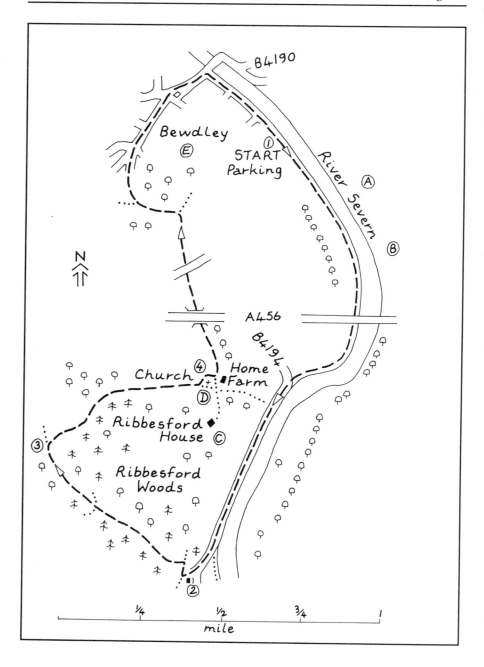

4. Leave the churchyard through the gate and turn left along a track, which goes under a road, following the blue Worcestershire Way waymarks. Cross a minor road and continue ahead. Ignore a track to your left over a cattle grid, signposted to Snuffmill Pool, and walk ahead for 30 yards (25m) to a little green wooden gate on your left. Go through it and follow the path. Go through a kissing gate and over a wooden foot-bridge to join Snuff Mill Walk. Turn right and walk downhill towards Bewdley church. Turn right at the bottom, then walk to the left of the church to return to the start.

Places of Interest

A. Although the River Severn appears quite wide here, shallows downstream inhibit any meaningful navigation much beyond Stourport these days. This was not always the case – there was once a regular trade to Bewdley and as far as Arley Quarry landing, some 5 miles (8km) to the north. Navigation was only possible when river levels were high, and the trade was recorded in 1904 as being 'very small'.

B. During the summer months, and on Spring and Autumn weekends, you will see puffs of steam and hear the whistles of the Severn Valley Steam Railway. This restored private line runs for 16 miles (26km) along the Severn Valley between Kidderminster and Bridgnorth, with trains of cream and brown carriages hauled by splendid green steam locomotives. There is a station at Wribbenhall, just across the river from Bewdley, so try to make time for a ride if you can. Telephone 0299 40316 for details, 0299 401001 for the 24-hour recorded timetable.

C. Ribbesford Manor House occupies a superb situation to the south of the church, and overlooking the river. Dating from the 16th century, many of its early features have been obscured by later additions. It is private.

D. St Leonard, the patron saint of prisoners, died in 559 AD at Noblac, France, after founding a monastery there. This church, dedicated to him, is Norman in origin, although the north aisle, north arcade and chancel were all rebuilt, following lightning damage during a terrible storm in June 1877. John Ruskin (1819-1900), who wrote about this kind of thing, commented that he would have preferred to let 'the dear old ruin grow grey by Severn's side in peace'. Most visitors today would certainly disagree with him, as there are a host of interesting features to enjoy.

St Leonard's most striking exterior feature is the timbered bell turret, which contains three bells, one of which is thought to have been cast in the early 13th century. Entry to the church is through a timber-framed porch (dating from 1633) and a Norman doorway, above which is a carving of a hunter in a full length tunic. To the right is the stained-glass west window, designed by Burne-Jones and made by William Morris in 1875. It depicts a beggar girl being given a new cloak. The window at the end of the south aisle contains fragments of very ancient glass, illustrating St George and the dragon.

The south aisle has a timber arcade dating from the 15th century, a feature thought to be unique in Britain. The north aisle occupies the site of the original Norman church. The pulpit incorporates 15th century wood carvings, taken from the rood screen. One depicts a pig blowing a bagpipe! As you leave the church through the churchyard, where heavily overgrown tombstones lean this way and that, you face a fine group of sandstone farm buildings. One of them, the long barn, probably dates from the 17th century.

E. Bewdley has been described as 'the most perfect small Georgian town in Worcestershire'. Its river frontage, bridge and broad main street remain substantially unspoiled, making it ideal for a ramble among the many handsome buildings, quaint shops and inviting old pubs.

It has been suggested that the name Bewdley may derive from 'Beau Lieu', a beautiful place. Certainly its situation, tucked in between a steep hillside and the River Severn, is splendid.

The town was granted its Charter by Edward IV in 1472. Prince Arthur lived at nearby Tickenhill Manor for a while, and married Catherine of Aragon (1485-1536, and later first wife of Henry VIII) in the town.

Bewdley was for many years the focal point of carrying on the River Severn, goods being brought to here, and beyond, in the wide, flat bottomed craft called Severn trows. This trade ended when the

Staffordshire & Worcestershire Canal was completed in 1772 (see Walk 23).

It is well worth crossing Telford's fine three-arched bridge, completed in 1798, to the Wribbenhall side of the river, for a view encompassing the whole of Bewdley's quayside, substantially unchanged since the 18th century. Then walk back across the bridge and up Load Street for a closer look at the Church of St Anne, which stands slightly skewed at the top. The tower dates from 1696, the rest from 1748. There is a museum in Butchers' Shambles, off Load Street, which includes a brass foundry and a saw pit (telephone 0299 403573, admission charge).

Walk 22:
Stourport &
Hartlebury Common

6 miles (9.7km). Strenuous

*To be walking through sand dunes, when so far from the sea, is an unusual
feature of this walk. They are to be found on Hartlebury Common, a superb
natural environment by the River Severn. This is followed by an exploration of
Stourport, a unique town in that it owes its existence solely to the construction
of a canal. Combined with gentle riverside and canal-side walking, this is a
stimulating and enjoyable ramble.*

The Route

1. Start from the car park at Hartlebury Common Local Nature Reserve,
   which is on the B4193 between Stourport and Hartlebury. Bus no 219
   from Stourport stops here (for information phone 0345 212555).

   Take the track immediately to the right of the sign to the picnic area,
   initially following blue waymarks. Continue ahead, always maintaining your position on the highest part of the ridge. As you start to
   descend, a main road comes in from the right. Ahead are two
   electricity pylons, close together. Pass these and then descend
   through trees to the road. Turn left to pass the Titton Inn. Walk along
   the road for about 300 yards (275m), then take the footpath signposted to Lincomb, on the right.

2. Climb up steps and continue with a wire fence on your left, to
   emerge at Titton Hill Farm. Turn right. The track soon bends to the
   left. Take the rough path behind the cottage, which descends through
   trees (some fallen) in a zigzag, and joins a lane. Maintain your
   direction, then take the first left along a track. Cross open ground to
   join a road on an industrial estate. Turn right and walk past factories
   on your left to a T-junction. Turn left. At the entrance to Severnside

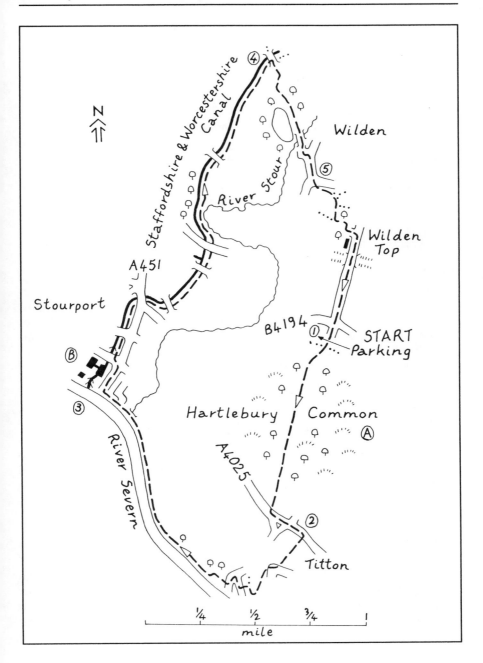

Caravan Park, follow the footpath sign into the park. Turn right and follow the park road, which turns left to a stile by the river. Cross it and walk with the water on your left.

3. When you reach the entrance lock to Stourport Basins, go to the right of the Tontine Hotel, up Mart Lane. Explore the basins, then return to your route. Pass Lichfield Street on the right, then, after about 20 yards (18m), you will see York Street Lock on your left. Join the canal here and walk with the water on your left.

4. At Oldington Bridge (a large pipe partially obscures the name) by a gas pumping station, you leave the canal by turning sharp right to follow the track. Pass Wilden Pool on your right, cross a bridge, and follow the road through a small industrial estate. You join a road and turn right.

5. Turn left at Bigbury Lane, then immediately walk to the right up a track signposted 'public footpath'. It soon becomes a path. When it forks, go to the right to join another path. Go right. You emerge at Wilden Cricket Club clubhouse. Walk to the left of this building, along the edge of the pitch, to a stile. Cross it and turn left to walk with the hedge on your right, until you reach a stile in the hedge. Cross it and walk to another stile across the field. Cross it and turn left along a lane. Turn right at the road to return to the start.

Places of Interest

A. Hartlebury Common is regarded by naturalists as one of the most important surviving areas of heathland in the West Midlands. It was thus recognised by the Nature Conservancy Council in 1955, when they designated it a Site of Special Scientific Interest. Originally owned by the Church Commissioners, it was purchased by the County Council in 1968, although they had managed it since 1957

Covering an area of 216 acres, and rising to a height of 184 feet (56m), it consists mainly of dry lowland or shrub heath on river terraces of sand over a bed-rock of Triassic sandstone. This sand has, in places, formed into dunes, which shift with the wind – a very rare feature so far inland.

There is a pond, and marshy patches, which support aquatic plants, dragonflies and frogs. Birds to look out for include long-tailed tits, tree pipits and stonechats. You may also find ling heather, bell heather, bogbean, marsh cinquefoil, heath milkwort and shepherds purse amongst the plant communities. There are dung beetles, green tiger beetles, large skipper butterflies, and common lizards. But don't spend all your time searching the undergrowth – the views are excellent.

Stourport

B. The Staffordshire & Worcestershire Canal Company did offer to have their canal join the River Severn at Bewdley, but the elders of that town declined. So the company chose a spot further downstream where the River Stour empties into the Severn, marked at that time by a lonely ale house. The canal was completed in 1772, and was an immediate success, feeding goods down from the Potteries to Gloucester and Bristol. The great canal basins built at Stourport needed houses, churches, pubs, hotels and many other amenities to support them. Thus the town of Stourport was built, the only such town in England that owes its existence solely to the construction of a canal.

Away from the canal the town, although pleasant, is of little interest. This walk takes you past all the significant buildings: the Tontine Hotel, built in 1788 by the canal company; Mart Lane, a fine terrace of cottages once threatened with demolition; and the central warehouse, with its clock tower. The basins are always packed with a variety of craft, and in summer there is a constant movement of boats through the locks. Take time to wander around and savour the atmosphere and quiet charm typical of 18th-century industrial and utilitarian buildings.

Walk 23:
Tardebigge

6.5 miles (10.5km). Moderate

The distinctive tower of the church at Tardebigge is a conspicuous landmark for miles around, so there is no problem in identifying the start of this walk. On the return, when climbing beside the many locks, spare a thought for the boatmen and women who once had to navigate their loaded pairs of narrowboats up and down the flight. Any romantic notions of their working lives should soon be dispelled.

The Route

1. Tardebigge is on the B4184, 2.5 miles (4km) from Bromsgrove. Turn off down the minor road to park by the church (avoid Sunday service times of 8am, 11am & 6.30pm). Bus numbers 319 & 321 between Redditch and Bromsgrove stop here (for information phone 0345 212555).

   Walk through the churchyard, passing a school on your left. Turn left to walk along the right-hand side of the playground to a stile, Cross it and turn right.

2. At the T-junction, continue straight ahead through a metal gate. Follow the track through another gate to pass Patchetts Farm on your right, ignoring a footpath signposted to the right after the farm.

3. Just past a house on your right, the main track turns to the right. Continue ahead, looking for a waymarked wooden gate to the right of the field entrance ahead. Go through the gate down an old hollow-way. You emerge at a road, where you go to the left. At the road junction, turn right towards Stoke Prior.

4. Turn right at Sugarbrook Lane, and join the canal at the bridge. Walk with the water on your left.

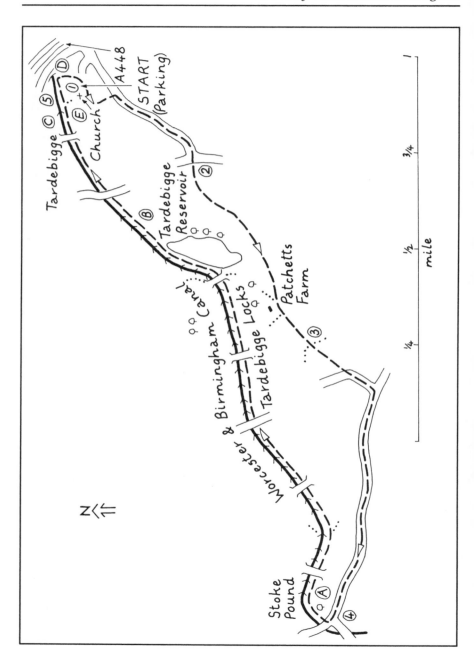

5. With the tunnel entrance in view, go through the kissing gate to the right, and follow the path, which is partially enclosed by railings. Enter the churchyard through a gate, to return to the start.

Places of Interest

A. This is the first of 30 narrow locks in the Tardebigge flight, which raise the canal 217 feet (66m). Just below the bridge are the six locks of the Stoke flight, which have a combined rise of 42 feet (12.8m).

B. This engine house used to pump water from the feeder reservoir, by the canal, to the summit level, 50 feet (15m) above. It is now a restaurant/disco.

C. Tardebigge Top Lock is one of the deepest narrow locks in the country, with a rise of 14 feet (4.2m). It replaced an earlier boat lift. Look for the plaque which commemorates the founding of the Inland Waterways Association by L.T.C. Rolt and Robert Aickman in 1946, aboard the narrowboat Cressy, moored here at the time.

D. The entrance to Tardebigge Tunnel, on the summit level. It is 580 yards (530m) long. The mellow buildings and warehouses to the left are a British Waterways Yard. There are often well preserved working narrowboats moored here.

E. Sited unashamedly on top of a hill 531 feet (162m) high, the needle spire of St Bartholomew's Church soars towards the heavens in spectacular style. Designed in 1777 by Frances Hiorn, it perches atop an airy Baroque bell chamber and slender tower. The rest of the building is, by contrast, quite unremarkable.

Walk 24:
Salwarpe and
The Droitwich Canals

4.5 miles (7.2km). Moderate

The Droitwich Canals, which link the River Severn with the Worcester &
Birmingham Canal, are currently undergoing steady restoration. Starting from
the sleepy village of Salwarpe, this route explores their various states:
overgrown and reed-bound; dredged but not yet navigable; and fully restored.

The Route

1. Salwarpe is on a minor road off the A38, close to its junction with the
    A4057 on the Worcester side of Droitwich. Park by the lych gate, in
    front of the church.

    With your back to the lych gate, walk to the right along the road.
    When the road turns to the right, continue ahead over a stile by a
    gate, and walk down the field to the left for about 50 yards (45m) to
    cross a stile. Turn right along the path. Cross two stiles in quick
    succession, and continue with a fence on your left. Cross another stile
    and walk towards a foot-bridge over to your right.

2. Cross the foot-bridge and walk over the brow of the field, veering
    slightly to the right. In the bottom corner, cross a fence stile and walk
    with a wire fence on your left. Join a lane and follow the sign to
    Hadley Heath. Turn left at the road, walk for about 25 yards (23m),
    then turn right through a metal gate. Turn sharp right and walk up
    the hill to the right of the trees. Follow the waymark posts, with the
    trees on your left. Look for a prominent gap in the hedge over to
    your right. Walk through it and continue with the hedge on your left.
    You arrive at a road through a gap in the hedge.

3. Turn left. Turn right at the T-junction and continue. When the road

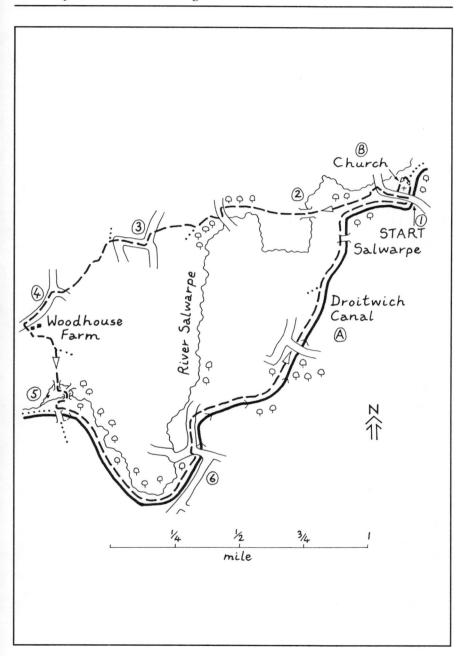

bends to the left, go through the waymarked gate on your right. At the metal gate ahead cross the stile on your left. Walk to a stile on the opposite side of the field, and cross it. Cross the stile ahead, then veer slightly left across a field to another stile, and cross it. Walk to the right through newly planted trees to cross a stile in the corner and emerge at a road. Turn right.

4. Turn left at the T-junction. Turn left at the signpost for the bridleway to Egg Lane. After about 20 yards (18m) fork left, following the waymark. Cross a foot-bridge and turn right. After about 50 yards (45m), take the right fork and walk with the hedge on your right. Go through a little metal gate and continue. Ignore a stile on your right to cross a gated foot-bridge ahead. Walk with a fence on your right.

5. You reach two foot-bridges. Take the black metal-gated foot-bridge on your right, and continue along the fenced track, which turns right and emerges at a gate by a disused lock. Turn left to join the canal and walk with the water on your right.

A restored section of the Droitwich Canal

6. At the first bridge, leave the canal through a gate. Turn left, then turn right along Porter's Mill Lane to rejoin the canal. Continue, passing several locks and bridges until you identify Salwarpe by noticing its square church tower ahead. Go under the large red-brick bridge at Salwarpe, and continue past the church until a path joins from the left. Turn sharp left up this path to enter the churchyard through a gate. Exit through the lych gate to return to the start.

Places of Interest

A. The Droitwich Barge Canal opened in 1771, and was finally abandoned in 1939. The Droitwich Junction Canal, linking the barge canal at Droitwich to the Worcester & Birmingham Canal at Hanbury, is narrow gauge. A Trust is working towards complete restoration of both.

B. The canal creeps through Salwarpe in a cutting, passing beneath the fine Church of St Michael. Built in Perpendicular style, parts of it are thought to date from around 1200.

Walk 25:
Worcester Cathedral

2.5 miles (4km). Easy

Starting from Worcester Bridge, this walk gives you the opportunity to make the most satisfactory approach to the great cathedral – from the river. There follows a short canal walk and an exploration of Diglis Basins, with the return being made alongside the Severn.

The Route

1. Start from Worcester Bridge, in the City of Worcester. There is a useful car park (charge) close to the bridge, and many buses.

   Walk along the South Quay towards the cathedral. Turn left at the sign post to the cathedral, walking through an archway and up steps. Go through another archway and up more steps, where the cathedral re-appears on your right. Turn right along the path towards the west window.

2. Walk around the left-hand side of the cathedral, through a metal gate, to emerge at a main road by the war memorial. Turn right and continue along College Street, crossing the road at the traffic lights to arrive at The Commandery and Civil War Centre. Turn left through the archway to join the canal at Sidbury Lock. Walk with the water on your right.

3. The canal widens at Diglis Basin. Follow the tow-path round to the left, then turn right to walk past Worcester Yacht Chandlers. Cross a swing foot-bridge and pass M. W. Marine on your left. Turn right to walk over another swing foot-bridge, to pass the lock-keepers house on your left. You arrive at Diglis Top Lock.

4. Turn left and walk down the tow-path, with the locks on your right, until you meet the river. Turn left, and walk with the river on your

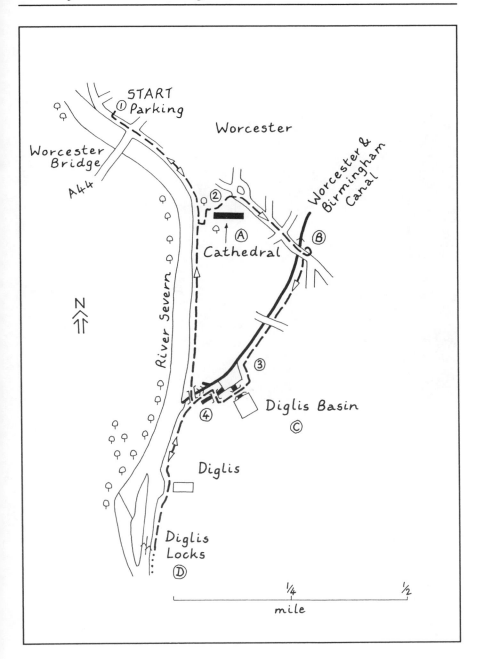

right. Continue, to reach Diglis Locks. Now initially retrace your steps, then continue always with the river on your left, to return to Worcester Bridge.

Always plenty to see at Diglis

Places of Interest

A. Hemmed in by a busy road on its eastern side, Worcester Cathedral is at its very best when viewed, and approached, from the river. The building has its origins in the 7th century, but was rebuilt by Bishop Oswald in 961, only to be ruined by the Danes 80 years later. St Wulstan, the only Saxon bishop at the time of the Norman Conquest, began building what we see today in 1084. The original tower fell in 1175, and was rebuilt in 1374. The exterior is now virtually all Victorian, so it is necessary to go inside to appreciate the finer early work.

B. The Commandery and Civil War Centre dates from the 15th century, and stands on the site of the Hospital of St Wulstan, founded in 1085, just outside the city walls. From the 13th century the masters of the hospital were referred to as commanders, hence the building's name. The building has a superb galleried hall and Elizabethan staircase. Open daily, closed Sunday mornings. Admission charge.

C. Diglis Basin is the terminus of the Worcester & Birmingham Canal, where it joins the River Severn. It is a fascinating area, packed with boats and nautical interest.

D. These massive locks on the river contrast starkly with the diminutive Sidbury Lock, beside The Commandery.

Walk 26: Knowle

4 miles (6.4km). Easy

A grand plan during the 1930s to modernise the canal link between London and Birmingham did little to encourage carrying on the canal. It did, however, leave us with some impressive flights of locks, and these at Knowle are an excellent example. The church, visited at the end of this walk, is a gem of a building.

The Route

1. Knowle is on the A41, about 3 miles (4.8m) from Solihull. You can park in the free car park signposted from the village centre, down St John's Close. There are plenty of buses (for information phone 021-200 2700).

   From the car park, turn right into St John's Close, with the green on your left. Continue ahead to a T-junction. Turn right into Lodge Road.

2. Cross the main A41 carefully, and continue ahead down Hampton Road. Cross the canal bridge and turn right down a path to the tow-path. Walk with the water on your right.

3. Go under bridge 70 and immediately turn left up to the road. Turn left and follow the road back to Knowle. Visit the church, then cross at the zebra crossing to return to the start along St John's Close.

Places of Interest

A. The remains of the original six narrow locks can be seen beside the impressive flight of five wide locks, which raise the canal 41 feet 10 inches (12.7m), built during the great modernisation of 1932. Note the

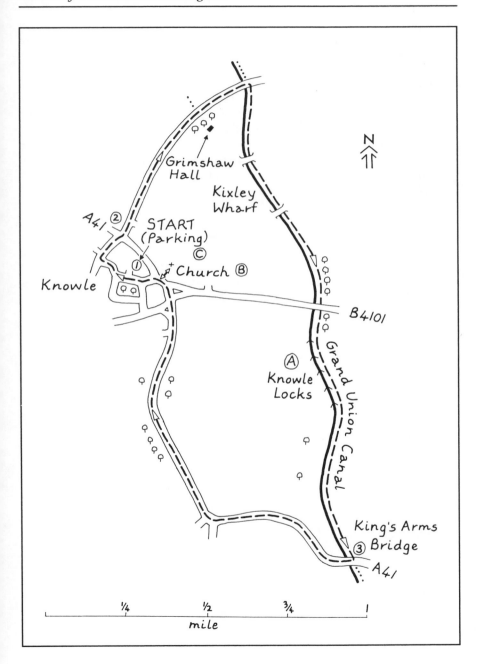

massive side ponds, built to save water, and the distinctive white caps on the ground puddles. These are the northernmost broad beam locks on the canal. Carrying continued, after modernisation, using paired narrowboats.

B. Knowle, a smart and sought-after village, is blessed with the exquisite parish Church of St John the Baptist, St Lawrence and St Anne. It was built as a result of the efforts of Walter Cook, a wealthy man who founded a chapel here in 1396, and completed the present church in 1402. Prior to this, the parishioners of Knowle had to make a 6 mile (9.7km) round trip each Sunday to the church at Hampton-in-Arden. This involved crossing the River Blythe, an innocuous brook today, but in medieval times 'a greate and daungerous water' which 'noyther man nor beaste can passe wt. owte daunger of peryshing'. The building is built in the Perpendicular style, with much intricate stonework. There is much of interest inside, including the roof timbers, the original font, and a medieval dug-out chest. The timbered Guild House, next to the church, was also built by Walter Cook.

C. This is the three-acre Children's Field, given to the National Trust in 1910 by the Rev. T. Downing, to be used for games.

Walk 27:
Kingswood Junction

3.8 miles (6.1km). Easy

Many of the typical features of the Stratford-on-Avon Canal – diminutive locks, split bridges, a barrel-roof cottage – are present on this gentle walk. You will also see a section of the Grand Union Canal, which, unlike its narrow neighbour, appears much more business-like and substantial.

The Route

1. Start from the picnic area by the canal in Lapworth, on the B4439, which is off the A34 at Hockley Heath. Those coming by train should turn right out of Lapworth station, and right again at the main road, to join the canal. There is a limited bus service from Warwick, for information phone 0926 495866.

   From the picnic area, walk with the canal on your left. Pass a lock and cross the little cast iron split-bridge, number 36, and continue with the water on your left. At the junction, do not cross bridge 37, but walk with the canal on your left towards Warwick.

2. Walk under bridge 63, turn right and walk up to the road. Turn left, then take the first right, to walk down Dick's Lane. The road deteriorates into a track by a barrel-roof cottage, and crosses the canal. At a T-junction, turn right, then after about 50 yards (45m), look for a stile on your left. Cross it and walk with the hedge on your right. When the hedge ends, maintain your direction to walk to the left of a thicket. Go through a waymarked gateway, keeping the trees to your right. Maintain your direction towards the motorway. Veer right to a stile.

3. Cross the stile, cross the road, and climb the stile opposite. Continue ahead. Go through a gap in a broken fence and walk to the hedge opposite. Turn right. Duck through a wire fence and continue to a

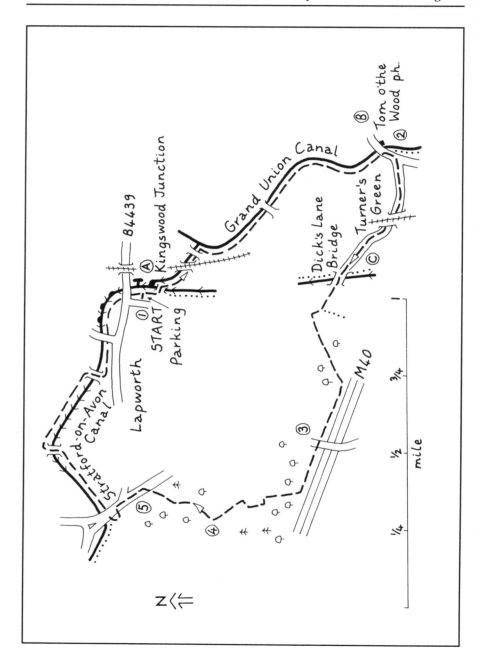

stile. Walk with the hedge, which is now on your right. Climb a fence stile and maintain your direction to a wooden gate.

4. Go through the gate, cross the stile ahead and follow the path to emerge at a road, over another stile. Cross the stile opposite and walk to the stile ahead. Cross it and continue along the path.

5. Turn left at the road, and left at the next T-junction. Join the canal at the bridge, and walk with the water on your left. The tow-path changes sides at the second lock, and back again at bridge 33. Return to the start just after bridge 35.

This fine sign still stands at Dick's Lane Bridge on the Stratford-on-Avon canal

Places of Interest

A. Kingswood Junction provides a link between the Stratford-on-Avon and Grand Union Canals. It is rich with interesting features such as a pretty lock cottage, a split bridge and a small canal maintenance yard.

B. This canalside pub, the Tom O' the Wood, takes its name from a windmill which once stood in the village.

C. Although much extended, if you look carefully you can identify the original 'barrel-roof' cottage, a design peculiar to this canal. These semi-circular roof frames were the same design as the supports used in the construction of brick-arched bridges. The cottage is private.

Walk 28:
The Hatton Flight

6 miles (9.7km). Moderate

There is some rich farmland to the west of Warwick – a landscape which epitomises the heart of England. This walk initially meanders past woods and through fields, to return down the dramatic Hatton Flight of locks on the Grand Union Canal. The panoramic view from the top is excellent.

The Route

1. This walk starts from the church car park in Budbrooke, which is signposted off the A41 at Hatton, not far from Warwick.

   From the car park, walk to the left along the road, then turn right into the waymarked track to Church Farm. Cross the stile on your left and walk across the field in the direction of the waymark. Cross a stile in the far corner and continue with the hedge on your left. Cross the foot-bridge in the corner, turn right and walk with the hedge on your right. Join a road by a large tree, and turn left.

2. At the road junction, turn right along the waymarked track, then by the ruined farm, go through a gap in the hedge to your left, and walk with the hedge on your right. Go around the field, following the waymarks. Emerge at a road and turn right. When the road splits, go to the left, by the woods.

3. Go through a metal gate to pass farm buildings on your right. Turn right by Wilderness Cottage, crossing a cattle grid and following the waymarked track. Cross another cattle grid and pass farm buildings on your right. Cross a third cattle grid and turn right through a metal gate. Walk ahead. Turn left at the hedge, staying in the same field.

4. Leave the field through the waymarked gap and continue with the hedge on your left. Cross a stile by a metal gate to join a road. Turn

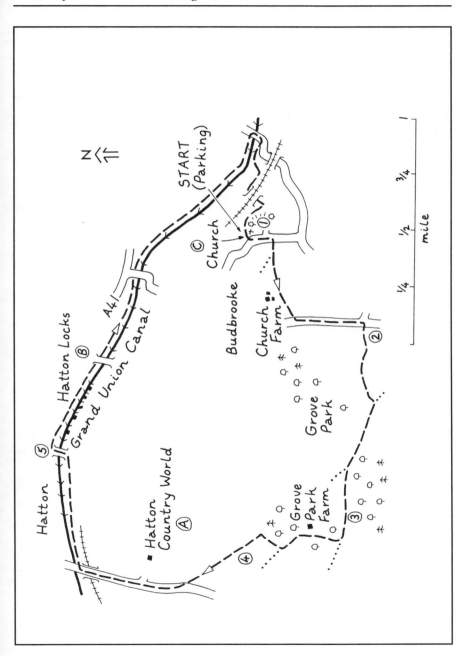

right. Join the canal at the bridge, turn right and walk with the water on your left towards Hatton Locks.

5. The tow-path changes sides by the old canal maintenance yard. Continue down to lock 27, where you cross the canal to take the footpath between posts opposite the bottom of the lock. You emerge at a road. Turn right and go through a wooden gate on your right. Walk along the right-hand side of the field, cross a foot-bridge over a ditch into the next field, and walk with the hedge on your left. Turn left under the railway, go through a metal gate and turn right. Walk towards the right-hand side of the church. Cross a stile at the end of the earthwork, and now walk towards the church. Cross another stile and follow the path. Walk through the churchyard to return to the car park.

Places of Interest

A. Hatton Country World has rare breeds, vintage farm machinery, craft workshops and many other attractions.

B. The Hatton Flight is one of the finest manifestations of the great Grand Union modernisation of 1930s. Note the distinctive caps on the ground paddle mechanisms, and the remains of the old narrow locks beside the newer wide ones.

C. Standing in a very tidy churchyard, St Michael's at Budbrooke has Norman and Early English origins, but has been extensively rebuilt. Its weather vane stands amongst the graves.

These distinctive covers on the ground paddle mechanisms at Hatton were part of the great 1930s modernisation

Walk 29:
Mary Arden's House

4 miles (6.4km). Easy

*Mary Arden's House is a well known attraction on the Shakespeare circuit.
As you walk around it, you will certainly rub shoulders with many other
visitors from all over the world. You can soon find peace and solitude, however,
if you follow this route through lush meadows and beside the pretty
Stratford-on-Avon Canal.*

The Route

1. This walk starts from Mary Arden's House in Wilmcote, which is clearly signposted off both the A34 and the A422, about 3 miles from Stratford-upon-Avon. Bus no 228 from Stratford stops in the village (for information phone 0788 535555), and the station is right by the canal bridge. There is a car park by the House, and roadside parking in the village.

   Walk past Mary Arden's House on your right, turn right at the T-junction, and take the public footpath on the right immediately after Glebe Farm. Walk to the left of the field, along the fenced path. Cross two stiles in quick succession and walk with the fence and hedge on your right.

2. Cross two more stiles and now walk with the hedge always on your left, crossing four more stiles, and then a metal gate to emerge at a lane. Turn right.

3. Turn right at the T-junction and follow the road. Turn right at the next T-junction.

4. Go under the aqueduct and immediately walk up steps to your right to join the canal. Explore the aqueduct, then walk with the water on your right. At the third bridge, by the Wilmcote Visitor Moorings, leave the canal to join the road. Turn right to return to the start.

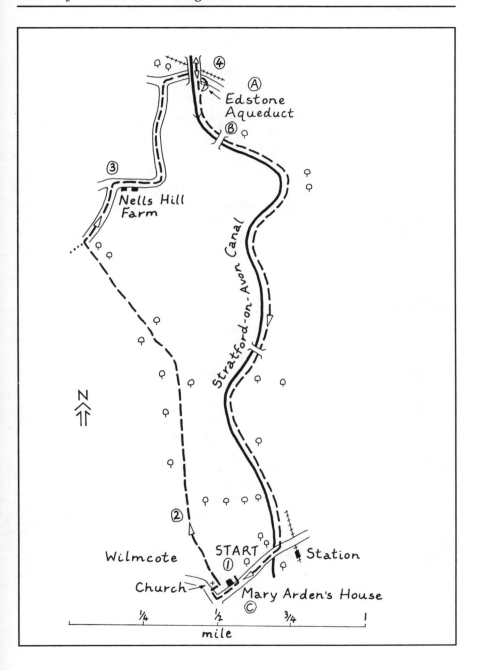

Places of Interest

A. Edstone (or Bearley) Aqueduct is the longest canal aqueduct in England. It carries the canal over a road, a railway, and a stream in a narrow cast-iron trough about 200 yards (185m) long, supported on brick piers. It is unusual in that the tow-path is at the level of the bottom of the tank, so walkers get a frog's eye view of any passing boat.

B. Draper Bridge is a 'split-bridge', typical of this canal. This one has subsided a little, and the gap in the arch has closed slightly. It was a clever design, which allowed the canal company to save on building costs. The line from the towing horse to the boat could be passed through the slit while the horse walked around the bridge. To take the tow-path through a bridge meant building a bigger arch, incurring more expense.

Mary Arden's House

C. Mary Arden's House in Wilmcote was the home of Shakespeare's mother. It is a beautifully preserved example of an early 16th-century farmhouse, and was indeed used as such until 1930, when it was purchased by the Shakespeare Birthplace Trust. Built with oak from the nearby Forest of Arden, it is of timber-frame construction with lime-plastered clay and wattle infill, standing on a stone foundation.

It is furnished as it would have been when occupied by a yeoman farmer in Shakespeare's time. A close inspection, with the help of the friendly guides, is both fascinating and instructive.

Mary Arden's House forms part of a larger estate including The Shakespeare Countryside Museum, where a collection of old farm implements, machinery and buildings are displayed. Open daily. Admission charge, café, shop. For information phone 0789 204016.

Walk 30:
Anne Hathaway's Cottage
& Shakespeare's Birthplace

6 miles (9.7km). Moderate

As one of Britain's major tourist venues, you can expect Stratford-upon-Avon to be busy and sometimes crowded. By following this route you will have a chance to enjoy a quiet walk beside the River Avon, and an entry into the town alongside the canal, as well as some of the major historic sights.

The Route

1. Start from the car park (charge) for Anne Hathaway's Cottage in Shottery, which is clearly signposted off both the A422 and the A439 on the edge of Stratford-upon-Avon. The Avon Shuttle bus from Stratford stops at the cottage (for information phone 0788 535555).

   Walk past the cottage on your left. Just after passing Burman's Farm on your left, look for a 'Cycling Prohibited' sign on your right, and walk down the path beside it. You cross a foot-bridge and come to a road, where you turn left. At the T-junction go straight across, following the public footpath to Wilmcote. Soon a tarmac path leads up to the left between houses. Follow this, turn left as you emerge, then right at the road junction.

2. Do not go to the left along Bishop's Close, but take the tarmac path to the right of the school playing fields. Pass the school, cross the road and follow the Shottery Brook, with the water on your right. When you have passed the last house on your left, go to the right up rough steps to join the canal. Walk with the water on your right.

3. Cross the canal carefully at the lock, using the handrail on the top gate, and then walk with the water on your right. After passing lock 52, leave the canal at bridge 65 to join a road. Walk to the right.

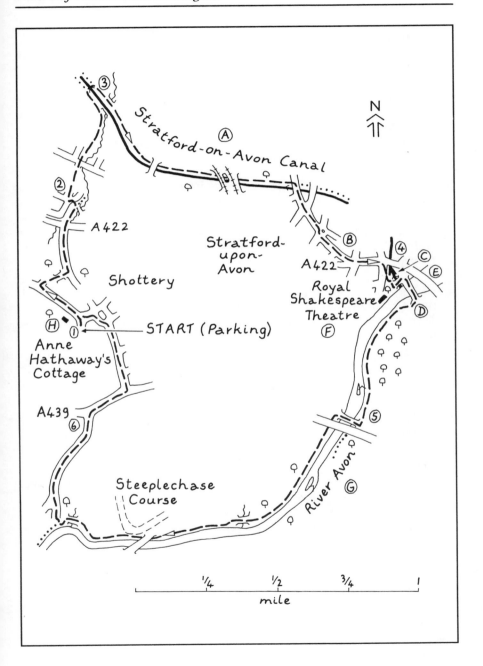

Continue ahead at the traffic lights. Turn right at a roundabout, then immediately left into Henley Street, a pedestrian precinct. Continue ahead towards the canal basin.

4. Cross the road at the pedestrian crossing and walk around the right-hand side of the basin. Cross the canal at the bridge by the entrance lock, and look for the red-brick Tramway Bridge over the River Avon, to your right. Cross it and walk with the river on your right, passing Colin P. Witter Lock.

5. Cross the foot-bridge (beside the road bridge) and now walk with the water on your left, passing through a squeeze stile just after the bridge. Continue, eventually crossing a stile, a foot-bridge with a stile, and another stile. Just after the next foot-bridge, by houses, the path splits. Turn sharp right and walk up to a cul-de-sac. Turn right. Emerge from Stannells Close and turn right.

6. At the end of Luddington Road, turn right at the main road. Turn left down Hathaway Lane, following signs to Anne Hathaway's Cottage. Turn left at The Bell pub, and left down Cottage Lane, to return to the start.

Places of Interest

A. Construction of the Stratford-on-Avon Canal began in 1793, but the whole route from King's Norton on the Worcester & Birmingham Canal to the River Avon at Stratford was not completed until 1815. After a short period of prosperity, the canal inevitably began to suffer from railway competition. In 1856 the company sold out to the Great Western Railway. There followed the usual steady decline and decay, with the last working boat on the southern section reaching Stratford in 1930, and only an occasional boat moving on the northern section in the 1950s.

In 1959 the National Trust leased the southern section, from Lapworth to Stratford, from the British Transport Commission. After over four years of restoration work, it was finally opened to navigation by Queen Elizabeth the Queen Mother on 11th July 1964.

On the 1st April 1988 control passed from the National Trust to British Waterways, who have the skill and resources to maintain it to the required standard. It is, without doubt, one of the prettiest of the waterways, and forms part of a popular cruising circuit which includes the rivers Avon and Severn, and the Worcester & Birmingham Canal.

B. Purchased as a memorial in 1847, this half-timbered house is where William Shakespeare was born in 1564. It is, of course, beautifully preserved and presented, and contains many Elizabethan and Jacobean furnishings.

William's father was a glovemaker, and part of the building consisted of a workshop used for this purpose. Somehow the building managed to survive the town fires which occurred around 1630.

Today, it is approached through a modern visitor centre, built in 1964, and a garden. Exhibits illustrate the bard's life. Open daily. Admission charge. For information phone 0789 204016.

C. To cope with the initial success of the canal, and the enormous quantity of goods and coal being brought into the town, there were once two basins, surrounded by wharfs and warehouses. One was levelled in 1901 to make space for the present gardens.

D. The narrow nine-arched Tramway Bridge, crossed on this walk, was built in 1823 to carry a horse-drawn tramway to Shipton-on-Stour.

E. Clopton Bridge was built 1480-90 by Sir Hugh Clopton, who became Lord Mayor of London in 1492. The second arch from the south end was damaged during the Civil War, and has been rebuilt. The toll house tower was added in 1814.

F. The Shakespeare Royal Theatre is a large, chunky, red-brick affair, designed by Elizabeth Scott and completed in 1932. Although quite radical at the time, it now appears rather dated. It is the home of the Royal Shakespeare Company. The first theatre in Stratford was a temporary octagon built for Garrick's Festival in 1769. It was not until 1827 that a permanent theatre was erected. A more substantial building followed in 1879, with a Library and Art Gallery being added in 1881. These survive, and are connected to the present building by a bridge.

G. Navigation on the Upper Avon ceased in 1875. The Upper Avon Navigation Trust, formed in 1965 under the leadership of David Hutchings MBE, campaigned and worked vigorously to enable its reopening on 1st June 1974.

H. A picturesque building of timber-frame and thatch, set in an old fashioned garden and orchard, Anne Hathaway's Cottage is all you would expect it to be. Anne married Shakespeare in 1582, and her family, yeomen farmers, continued in occupation until 1892, when the cottage was purchased by the Shakespeare Birthplace Trust. The rooms still retain their original features. Open daily, closed Sunday mornings, November to March. Admission charge. For information phone 0789 204016.

Anne Hathaway's Cottage – "Gee, ain't that the cutest!"

We publish a wide range of other titles, including general interest publications, guides to individual towns, and books for outdoor activities centred on walking and cycling in the great outdoors throughout England and Wales. This is a recent selection:

Cycling with Sigma ...

CYCLE UK! The Essential Guide to Leisure Cycling
— Les Lumsdon *(£9.95)*

OFF-BEAT CYCLING & MOUNTAIN BIKING IN THE PEAK DISTRICT
— Clive Smith *(£6.95)*

MORE OFF-BEAT CYCLING IN THE PEAK DISTRICT
— Clive Smith *(£6.95)*

50 BEST CYCLE RIDES IN CHESHIRE
— edited by Graham Beech *(£7.95)*

CYCLING IN THE LAKE DISTRICT
— John Wood *(£7.95)*

CYCLING IN SOUTH WALES
— Rosemary Evans *(£7.95)*

CYCLING IN THE COTSWOLDS
— Stephen Hill *(£7.95)*

BY-WAY BIKING IN THE CHILTERNS
— Henry Tindell *(£7.95)*

Country Walking ...

RAMBLES IN NORTH WALES — Roger Redfern
HERITAGE WALKS IN THE PEAK DISTRICT — Clive Price
EAST CHESHIRE WALKS — Graham Beech
WEST CHESHIRE WALKS — Jen Darling

WEST PENNINE WALKS – Mike Cresswell

STAFFORDSHIRE WALKS – Les Lumsdon

NEWARK AND SHERWOOD RAMBLES – Malcolm McKenzie

NORTH NOTTINGHAMSHIRE RAMBLES – Malcolm McKenzie

RAMBLES AROUND NOTTINGHAM & DERBY – Keith Taylor

RAMBLES AROUND MANCHESTER – Mike Cresswell

WESTERN LAKELAND RAMBLES – Gordon Brown *(£5.95)*

WELSH WALKS: Dolgellau and the Cambrian Coast
– Laurence Main and Morag Perrott *(£5.95)*

WELSH WALKS: Aberystwyth and District
– Laurence Main and Morag Perrott *(£5.95)*

WEST PENNINE WALKS – Mike Cresswell

CHALLENGING WALKS IN NORTH-WEST BRITAIN – Ron Astley *(£9.95)*

WALKING PEAKLAND TRACKWAYS – Mike Cresswell *(£7.95)*

– all of the above books are currently £6.95 each, except where indicated

If you enjoy walking 'on the level', be sure to read:

MOSTLY DOWNHILL, Leisurely Walks in the Lake District

MOSTLY DOWNHILL, Leisurely Walks in the White Peak

MOSTLY DOWNHILL, Leisurely Walks in the Dark Peak

Easy, enjoyable walking books; all £6.95

Long-distance walks:

For long-distance walks enthusiasts, we have several books including:

THE GREATER MANCHESTER BOUNDARY WALK – Graham Phythian

THE THIRLMERE WAY – Tim Cappelli

THE FURNESS TRAIL – Tim Cappelli

THE MARCHES WAY – Les Lumsdon

THE TWO ROSES WAY – Peter Billington, Eric Slater,
Bill Greenwood and Clive Edwards

THE RED ROSE WALK – Tom Schofield

FROM WHARFEDALE TO WESTMORLAND:
Historical walks through the Yorkshire Dales – Aline Watson

THE WEST YORKSHIRE WAY – Nicholas Parrott

– all £6.95 each

The Best Pub Walks!

Sigma publish the widest range of "Pub Walks" guides, covering just about every popular walking destination in England and Wales. Each book includes 25–30 interesting walks and varied suitable for individuals or family groups. *The walks are based on "Real Ale" inns of character and are all accessible by public transport.*

Areas covered include

Cheshire • Dartmoor • Exmoor • Isle of Wight • Yorkshire Dales • Peak District • Lake District • Cotswolds • Mendips • Cornwall • Lancashire • Oxfordshire • Snowdonia • Devon

… and dozens more—all £6.95 each!

General interest:

THE INCREDIBLY BIASED BEER GUIDE — Ruth Herman
This is the most comprehensive guide to Britain's smaller breweries and the pubs where you can sample their products. Produced with the collaboration of the Small Independent Brewers' Association and including a half-price subscription to The Beer Lovers' Club. *£6.95*

DIAL 999 — EMERGENCY SERVICES IN ACTION — John Creighton
Re-live the excitement as fire engines rush to disasters. See dramatic rescues on land and sea. Read how the professionals keep a clear head and swing into action. *£9.95*

THE ALABAMA AFFAIR — David Hollett
This is an account of Britain's rôle in the American Civil War. Read how Merseyside dockyards supplied ships for the Confederate navy, thereby supporting the slave trade. The *Alabama* was the most famous of the 'Laird Rams', and was chased half way across the world before being sunk ignominiously. *£9.95*

PEAK DISTRICT DIARY — Roger Redfern
An evocative book, celebrating the glorious countryside of the Peak District. The book is based on Roger's popular column in *The Guardian* newspaper and is profusely illustrated with stunning photographs. *£6.95*

I REMAIN, YOUR SON JACK — J. C. Morten (edited by Sheila Morten)
A collection of almost 200 letters, as featured on BBC TV, telling the moving story of a young soldier in the First World War. Profusely illustrated with contemporary photographs. *£8.95*